BS.
680.
.W7
P47x

‖‖‖ ‖‖‖ ‖‖‖‖‖ ‖‖ ‖ ‖‖ ‖ ‖‖ ‖‖‖‖‖‖‖‖‖‖ ‖‖‖ ‖‖‖

S0-ADW-758

# PERSPECTIVES ON FEMINIST HERMENEUTICS

**Gayle Gerber Koontz and Willard Swartley, Editors**

BIP-96

*Occasional Papers No. 10*

Institute of Mennonite Studies
3003 Benham Avenue
Elkhart, Indiana 46517

GOSHEN COLLEGE LIBRARY
GOSHEN, INDIANA

## POLICY STATEMENT FOR THE <u>OCCASIONAL</u> PAPERS

<u>Occasional Papers</u> is a publication of the Institute
of Mennonite Studies and authorized by the Council
of Mennonite Seminaries (CMS). The four sponsoring
seminaries are Eastern Mennonite Seminary (Harri-
sonburg, Virginia), Goshen Biblical Seminary and
Mennonite Biblical Seminary (Elkhart, Indiana), and
the Mennonite Brethren Biblical Seminary (Fresno,
California). The Institute of Mennonite Studies is
the research agency of the Associated Mennonite
Biblical Seminaries.

<u>Occasional Papers</u> is released several times yearly
without any prescribed calendar schedule. The
purpose of the <u>Papers</u> is to make various types of
essays available to foster dialogue in biblical,
theological and practical ministry areas and to
invite critical counsel from within the Mennonite
theological community. While most essays will be
in finished form, some may also be in a more
germinal stage—released especially for purposes of
testing and receiving critical feedback. In
accepting papers for publication, priority will be
given to authors from the CMS institutions, the
Bible and religion faculties in the Council of
Mennonite Colleges, the Associate membership of the
Institute of Mennonite Studies, and students and
degree alumni of the four seminaries.

Orders for <u>Occasional Papers</u> should be sent to the
Institute of Mennonite Studies, 3003 Benham Avenue,
Elkhart, IN 46517.

Editor:  Willard M. Swartley, Director
         Institute of Mennonite Studies
Associate Editor:
         Elizabeth G. Yoder, Assistant Director
         Institute of Mennonite Studies

©1987, Institute of Mennonite Studies
ISBN 0-936273-10-0
Printed in U.S.A.

# CONTENTS

8-16-90

BIB/DYN

# PREFACE

The essays in this collection might be considered bubbles simmering visibly on the surface of
a pot of stew. They arise from many hours of study
and conversation with and among those in various
parts of the United States and Canada who respect
both the Bible and feminist conviction.

While the stewpot includes ingredients from
Massachusetts and Colorado, Alberta and Manitoba,
Minnesota and Tennessee, some of the simmering took
place on the campus of the Associated Mennonite
Biblical Seminaries in Elkhart, Indiana, in 1986.
During the month of June and with the support of
the Institute of Mennonite Studies, three con-
tributors to this volume, Mary Schertz, David
Schroeder and Willard Swartley joined several other
researchers exploring the theme of shalom in the
portions of the Scripture in which they had been
doing scholarly work. Near the end of the month a
group of thirty predominantly Mennonite women were
invited to campus for two days to serve as con-
sultants for these biblical scholars on the theme
of feminist hermeneutics.

Most of the following essays were part of the
mix at this two-day consultation. The responses
written by Swartley and Ollenburger to the Bible
studies were solicited later to encourage further
conversation. In addition to Mennonite women
engaged at various levels of biblical and theological studies, several invited guests from other
Christian traditions brought their experience and
scholarly tools to the consultation on biblical
hermeneutics in feminist perspective. Catherine
Clark Kroeger, an evangelical Christian feminist
educated as a classicist, offers, in the initial
essay in this collection, a novel perspective on I
Corinthians 14:34-35 based on her research on the
sacred cries of women in Greco-Roman cults.
Toinette Eugene, a Catholic "woman of color" teaching at Colgate-Rochester Divinity School, calls for
care in analyzing social as well as theological
realities in our lives, and argues that a feminist
biblical hermeneutics "must remain an essential and
critical component of any theology of liberation."

The remaining essays in the first section of
the book deal in one way or another with the

5

"authority" of Scripture in relation to feminist
experience and commitments. David Schroeder
briefly outlines his understanding of the relationship of Bible, revelation, and community and notes
some of the implications for translating and interpreting Scripture which follow if one takes
seriously the new question raised by feminists--
What was the world of experience of women in biblical times? Mary Schertz struggles with the perceived forced choice in some cases between the
authority of the text and the authority of women's
experience, and suggests that the tension between
these two authorities can be reconceived not as an
"unconquerable obstacle" but as a "possibility for
the creation of meaning."

Diane MacDonald, utilizing the work of Hans-
Georg Gadamer and Gordon Kaufman, criticizes Mennonites who take an "objectivist stance to the biblical writings that tries to uncover the truth of
equality in every text," calling instead for a perspective that "recognizes truth as inter-subjective
and open-ended." Lydia Harder explores how the
shape of the hermeneutic community, a question
important both to many Anabaptist/ Mennonites and
to many contemporary Christian feminists, is challenged by feminist analysis of traditions, communal
structures, institutions and language.

The second portion of the book, a series of
four Bible studies presented at the consultation,
can be described as different attempts by biblical
scholars to interpret and appropriate biblical
materials in relationship to feminist consciousness. As Schertz points out in her first attempt,
the studies fit into the descriptive categories
outlined by Katharine Sakenfeld: 1) the study on
Luke 19:28-21:38 looks "to the Bible generally for
a theological perspective offering a critique of
patriarchy"; 2) both Schroeder's work on the
Haustafeln and Schertz's study of I Peter 2:11-5:11
look "to texts about women to counteract famous
texts 'against' women"; 3) the fourth study on
Judges 11:29-40 looks "to texts about women to
learn from the intersection of history and stories
of ancient and modern women living in patriarchal
cultures." The respondents assess the interpretive
moves of the writers and the theological use they
make of the texts.

While this collection of papers can serve to encourage further Mennonite evaluation and appropriation in various geographic areas of the contributions of feminist hermeneutics to biblical studies, the 1986 consultation itself highlighted some of the hindrances to a "well-cooked stew."

1) Ambivalence about involvement in the enterprise itself. This consultation, to my knowledge, was the first to draw together Anabaptist-Mennonite women with post-M.A. or M.Div. education in biblical and theological studies for face-to-face conversation. The women able to converse freely in the language and argumentation of these disciplines are few (actually a minority of the participants) and the personal connections between us are fledgling. There is disagreement among feminists, which was reflected among and within participants at the consultation, about the value of academic training, at least in traditional patterns. Is investment in doctoral studies a priority for committed Christian feminists? Does a feminist "shalom theology" rather call for more active lives of reconciliation than academic environments encourage or require? To what extent are those working in academic modes examples of co-opted energy and to what extent are they sisters in the work of redemption?

2) Uncertainty about who to fruitfully include in the conversation. The consultation's language and planning reflected continuing confusion about the relationship of "feminist" and "women's" perspectives. The two terms are not synonymous. Feminism is a particular way of seeing or interpreting reality and responding to it which involves 1) the naming and rejection of sexism against women and 2) as many feminists further define it, the affirmation of and action promoting the fundamental equality of men and women, equitable sharing, and mutuality between women and men. A "feminist" point of view cannot be equated flatly with a "woman's" view. Women's experience and convictions, especially when one considers women of various races, classes and cultures, are highly diverse. While feminists are interested in paying attention to distinctive women's experience and psychology resulting from biological differences (menstruation, childbearing, nursing, menopause)

and at the experiences women along with other
devalued persons have had when they have been
socially marginalized, feminist consciousness is
centrally concerned with how we as men and women
perceive and attach significance to our biological
differences in specific social and cultural worlds.
Christian feminist scholars in biblical, historical
and theological studies look specifically at the
way such significances attached in our religious
worlds of meaning and acting. This definition
indicates that men as well as women can be feminist
or sexist or somewhere in between.

The work of assessing and appropriating the
contributions of feminist hermeneutics can best be
done not by women qua women, but 1) at a practical
level by the church as a whole, and 2) at a
scholarly level by those familiar with and having
some expertise in Christian feminist work and biblical studies (although I would assume that at this
point the majority of the group would be, and in
any case at least half of the group should be
women).

Here the ambivalence surfaces more clearly. On
the one hand more intentional location of and participation by feminist men and men familiar with
the work of feminist scholars would have been
appropriate and could have strengthened cross-
gender collegiality at the consultation. On the
other hand, adding more men to the group would
likely have negatively affected the participation
of women, and hearing women's responses to feminist
hermeneutics was one primary purpose for the consultation.

A further ambivalence is related to the importance of feminist commitment. Is feminist consciousness and commitment negotiable? Can the word
of God be clearly heard (or interpreted) among
those who are not feminists? Is evaluation of the
contributions of feminist hermeneutics best done by
sympathetic Christian feminists (both male and
female) or in working groups where there are those
who have both positive and negative responses to
feminist scholarship? If plural views are inten-
tionally present in a Christian consultation, it
seems to me important that those expressing differing points of view should have a relatively even
balance of "power," or that special care be taken

to respect and account for minority perspectives.
In such cases a spirit and plan of interaction must
be fostered which allows for fuller than usual
hearing of the experiences which lie behind each
other's convictions. The consultation did not
clearly model this kind of interaction.

   3) The typical structure of consultations. A
number of the participants noted that the structure
of the consultation--presentations of papers and
large group discussion morning, afternoon and
evening--did not take adequate account of feminist
analysis and commitments in relation to the
dynamics of male/female psychology and interaction
(the fears of many women about speaking in large
groups, the hesitation of some men to speak freely
in a consultation on feminist hermeneutics); in
relation to the importance of caring for the body
as well as for the mind (long sitting days); in
relation to the value of committing time to building relationships beyond that which occurs during
focused large group meetings as such time aids both
intellectual work and group process; in relation to
the importance of drawing into public theological
conversation participants' own experiences of
sexism (also racial and class discrimination) as
well as liberation from these.

   In addition to the essays themselves, such
retrospective considerations from one layer of the
many conversations which lie beneath the surface of
this collection, can help us understand and shape
the future interpretive communities who will continue to assess feminist contributions to biblical
hermeneutics.

                              Gayle Gerber Koontz
                              October, 1987

PART 1:   FEMINIST HERMENEUTICS


A CLASSICIST LOOKS AT THE "DIFFICULT" PASSAGES

## Catherine Clark Kroeger

Over forty years ago, as a student at Bryn Mawr
College, I began my quest into the will and Word of
God for women. It was my conviction that God did
not give women brains, gifts, and talents and then
forbid their use in church or society. Very early
I encountered the writings of Katherine Bushnell,
who insisted passionately that it was not the Bible
which was repressive of women but rather the translations and interpretations of it. She upheld the
full authority and inspiration of the Scriptures
but insisted that within them lay a manifesto of
women's liberation. Hers was not the only voice to
cry out against the manipulation of the Bible to
oppress women. Sarah Grimke protest against "the
false translations of some passages by the MEN who
did that work, and against the perverted interpretations of the MEN who undertook to write com-
mentaries thereon." She went on to say, "I am
inclined to think when we are admitted to the honor
of studying Greek and Hebrew we shall produce some
various readings of the Bible, a little different
from those we have now."[1]
Out of this tradition I returned to graduate
school after twenty-five years. The good news was
that Greek and Latin hadn't changed much. My first
objective was to gain a mastery of Greek which
would enable me to grapple with the difficult New
Testament passages relevant to women. I was committed to the Bible as our only infallible rule of
faith and practice, but I intended to subject it to
the scrutiny of a feminist eye. I would look for
alternative translations and understandings which
did not do violence to the authority of Scripture
nor to the integrity of women. Admittedly this is
a subjective exercise, but the quest is imperative.
This scrutiny of the Greek texts did indeed
yield some remarkable material, but increasingly I


1.  As quoted in Aileen S. Kraditor ed., Up from
the Pedestal:   Landmark Writings in the American
Women's Struggle for Equality. Chicago: Quad-
rangle Books, 1968, p. 54.

began to look at the world of ancient women and
their religions. I studied monumental evidence
such as inscriptions, vase paintings, tomb paint-
ing, coins, and papyri as well as the more conventional classical texts. All of these sources are
necessary to study the lives of the women in antiq-
uity because ordinary history is written by, for,
and about men. The evidence for women must be
painstakingly pieced together from many quarters.

Classical studies, the recovery of the culture
of the Greco-Roman world, was in the last century a
basic component in an understanding of the world
into which the Apostle Paul moved. Since the
beginning of the century, there has been a bifurca-
tion of the two disciplines, indeed often a mutual
hostility between New Testament and classical
studies. A fusion of these disciplines is essential if we are to understand the dictates of the
Apostle to the Gentiles as he wrote to women newly-
converted from paganism.

You are kind to ask a classicist to join your
deliberations on this subject. As such, my contribution must be at a very elementary level, in
fact, at the ground floor. I begin by asking, "Is
the textual tradition reliable?" Gordon Fee,
formerly of Gordon-Conwell Seminary, tells me that
the textual evidence convinces him that 1 Cor.
14:34-35 is a later interpolation. In the process,
we must first satisfy ourselves that we are working
with a reliable text.

Second we ask, "What does the text say?" Is it
accurately translated, or does the original language allow other meanings? Is the translation
tarnished by prejudice? Few versions, for instance, admit that the apostle mentioned in Romans
16:7 is a woman, Junia. Ordinarily the name is
changed to a masculine form, or else if she is
allowed to continue as a woman, it is simply said
that the apostles know her. In the same chapter
Phoebe is called a minister or deacon, though this
usually comes through in translation as "servant."
We must also ask whether extraneous matter has been
introduced into the translation. A case in point
would be 1 Corinthians 11:10 which literally says
that a woman ought to have power over her own head.
It is almost impossible to find a standard version
which gives this rendition. Archbishop Moulton

declared it to be one of the most difficult passages in the entire New Testament. Katharine Bushnell snorted that anyone with a single year of
Greek ought to be able to handle it adequately.
The language was perfectly straight-forward but
unacceptable to most translators.

Next comes the matter of language. Is there
more than one meaning for some of the words
employed in the passage? If there are other established meanings for a given term, what sense would
their utilization give to the passage? The verb
hupotasso, for instance, has a number of meanings,
as even the most conservative biblical dictionary
will admit. These dictionaries will carefully
point out, however, that when applied to women, the
verb means that they should obey their husbands.
The word "silence" has at least five different
meanings in the New Testament in particular and in
Greek religion as a whole. Do we give any indication of this in the passages dealing with women?

Recently there has been much controversy over
kephale, the word for head. Traditionalists deny
that it has in the Greek the value of origin or
source, and yet the ancients believed that human
sperm was lodged in the head. It passed down the
spinal chord and passed on to bring new life into
the world. Artemidorus of Daldo wrote that just as
the father is the source of life for the son, so
the head is the source of life for the body. Sometimes the statue of a bearded head was set at the
source of a river, for the rest of the body flowed
forth from the head. To insert the notion of
source and supplier of life into the headship passages such as Ephesians 5 and 1 Corinthians 11
brings a very different understanding to the relationship between husband and wife.

Then there is the matter of grammar. Is there
an unexpected construction which might give another
interpretation? The Greek of Romans 16:2 may be
understood to say that Phoebe was an overseer who
had been ordained by Paul himself. The very same
construction is used to say that Paul was made or
ordained a minister. Why, then, are we so reluc-
tant to give the same rendering when it refers to a
woman rather than a man?

That bane of our existence, 1 Timothy 2:12 can
be construed as an indirect statement with a

redundant negative so that the emphasis is upon
<u>what</u> women are forbidden to teach rather than upon
their teaching or administrative function. We need
also to be aware that New Testament writers did not
always adhere to the forms of pure Attic. Indeed,
most of these authors did not use Greek as their
mother tongue, and some of their usages defy the
orderly rubrics of the grammarians. Even a native
Greek may lead one to despair, however. Perhaps
you remember the old rhyme:

> Polyphoisboisterous Homer of old
> Threw all his augments into the sea,
> Although he had often been courteously told
> That perfect imperfects begin with an e.
> But the Poet replied with a dignified air,
> "What the digamma does any one care?"

All of this presupposes a knowledge of Greek, a
prospect which fills many women with terror. I
believe that many subtle influences have been used
to deflect women from a serious study of the language. In this way they are disbarred from coming
to terms with the text.

If the text is important, so too is context.
How often we seize upon an isolated verse and
forget its provenance. Let us take an instance,
the troubled situation in the Corinthian church,
where many members of the congregation had recently
been led astray by dumb idols. In other words,
they were recent converts from heathenism. The old
attitudes and practices to which the new Christians
still subscribed were a serious problem. They
became drunk in honor of Jesus, as they had before
unto Dionysos. They still attended meals in the
idols' temple, engaged in ritual cursing and
fornication, and brought ecstatic elements into the
staid pattern of Jewish worship.

It is in this context that I believe we should
understand 1 Corinthians 14:34-35. The major
emphasis is upon noise control. Everyone is talking at once, and there is much sound but little
meaning. It was precisely this sort of confused
uproar which was so important in some of the pagan
cults. The Apostle asks that all utterances be
interpreted in a meaningful fashion and that if
there is no one to give sense to the utterance,

then the speaker is to remain silent. Similarly,
those who communicate meaning may speak only one at
a time so that everyone may understand the import
of the message. If someone else wishes to express
a thought from God, the first speaker must be
silent.

There is a third command relating to silence,
but this one draws much attention since it is
addressed to women. I suggest that the directive
refers to a type of utterance which was peculiarly
the province of women. In the Greco-Roman cults of
which I have been speaking, the fair sex was
expected to provide not meaning but noise. From
the time of Homer onward, we read of the sacred
cries of women. These ululations formed a significant part of Greek religious practice. Their
importance at Corinth has been demonstrated by the
discovery of a plaque dedicated to the sacred cries
of women. But the phenomenon persists to this very
day among rural Greek women. I suggest that Paul's
command was intended to deal with the continuing
problem of too much noise and too little meaning.
Women were not to ululate during divine services,
although they were free to pray and prophesy provided their heads were covered.

It is here that an understanding of the
cultural and religious context of the Greco-Roman
world becomes crucial. We are well acquainted with
the facts of male cults and of the prohibitions
which Paul gave to new believers: "Do not walk any
longer as the heathen do" (Eph. 4:17). "Do not
engage in drunken orgies in honor of the pagan
gods" (Rom. 13:13). But the cults of women were
distinctively different. Women frequently wor-
shipped different gods in different temples on different festival days and with different modes.
Women were noisy and abandoned while men were
sedate and maintained an auspicious silence. Women
made the most of religious events which gave them
license to leave their homes, and they were often
accused of going to rather drastic extremes. The
religious practices of women in the ancient world
were often indecent, indecorous and indiscreet.
Men feared their rites, hated them, derided them,
and repudiated them. What happened when pagan
women were converted and incorporated into the wor-
shipping body of Jesus Christ?

Only in the last twelve years or so has the subject of women's cult activities been of any real interest to scholars. How can we understand the decrees of the missionary to the Gentiles if we do not understand the mores of pagan women? Have we asked the right questions when we come to the difficult and seemingly oppressive passages in the Bible? Let us walk with faith as we use our scholarly tools to seek positive and creative answers.

# BIBLICAL INTERPRETATION

## David Schroeder

In the task of interpreting the Bible, I begin with the presupposition that there is a revelation of God's character in history, and that this revelation is reflected in the Bible. What are some of the implications of this presupposition for biblical interpretation?

First, let me make some comments about the experience reflected in the Bible:

1. It reflects the experience of the person who received the original revelation (e.g. Abraham).

2. It reflects the experience of the community that retained the witness of the revelation. Not all of it has remained.

3. It reflects the experience of the ones who in subsequent years interpreted the tradition and embedded it in their own witness to the work of God in history (e.g. JEDP documents).

4. It reflects the experience of the person(s) who put it into a larger collection or context (e.g. the Pentateuch).

5. It reflects the experience of the community that preserved and canonized the document.

6. It reflects the experience of the people who interpreted the canonic works over a long period of time (e.g. the Rabbinic and Quamran Literature).

7. It reflects the experience of the persons who used this material in New Testament times (Jesus, Paul, the Evangelists).

In addition, we can find help from all those throughout history who have interpreted the Scriptures before us--both the Old and the New Testament. Their experience is important to us in our understanding of the text and of God's revelation to humankind.

Second, I would like to make some general suggestions regarding interpretation:

1. We need to differentiate between the given socio-cultural context of the time of the revelation or writing and the revelation itself. The revelation of God is always given in and through a given culture or setting.

2. We need to understand the nature of theological language. Theological language has most often developed from straightforward reports

about significant revelatory events. In time,
however, specific words are filled with specific
theological significance and meaning. They become
technical terms. For example, at first the good
news that the man Jesus is the Christ was
proclaimed. Later the words for "good news" came
to stand for the Gospel of Jesus Christ.

3. There is progression of understanding of
God's revelation to humankind. The initial revelation sets a new direction toward life (often
against the prevailing culture, see 1. above).
This understanding is built on and added to in subsequent revelation.

4. The new revelations of God and God's will
come to us in the form of a promise, not as knowledge in hand. The promise of God as received by us
has to be responded to in faith in order for us to
experience the truth of the promise. When signs of
fulfillment appear we receive confirmation of the
truth of the promise. Thus the subjective and
objective aspects of revelation cannot be separated.

5. Through the record of the revelatory events
experienced (the canon) and the history of its
interpretation, we share with the people of God,
past and present, the knowledge of the character
and will of God. We thus need to continue to
reflect on the meaning of the text and its tradition; we need to interpret it for our time; we need
to find in and through it the promise for us today;
we need to commit our lives to the promise we perceive to be of God; we need to look over our
shoulders to see if God is blessing what we have
perceived to be God's will.

6. We can come to the text in two ways: 1) We
can move from the text to the present and let the
word speak to our present life, its values, temptations and opportunities or 2) we can move from crucial questions, crises and concerns of our day to
the text, to see if we can find parallel situations
that will speak instructively to our needs.

7. We cannot hope to find a purely objective
interpretation of Scripture. If we do, it will be
some form of legalism and will be impersonal, that
is, it will be contrary to the character of God.
We always bring to the Scriptures a pre-
understanding. Often this pre-understanding takes

us captive in such a way that it prevents us from
receiving what the text has to say. For example,
if we assume that a reference to the family in
Scripture refers to the nuclear family, then we
will not read it in terms of the extended family.
We are then held captive by a kind of eisegesis:
reading something into the text so we can read it
out of the text.

8. Because there is no purely objective interpretation we need to help each other to make proper
interpretations--we need an interpretive community.
The church, rather than the academic community, is
such a community of interpretation. This is done
through a process of loosing and binding under the
Spirit of God. It is a process of helping each
other to be loosed or liberated from the princi-
palities and powers that lead to death and to be
bound to those things we have discerned to be
actions that lead to life. Thus the interpretation
is with the understanding as well as with the
body--that is, through obedience to the promise
received.

With these thoughts in mind, let us turn our
attention to feminist interpretation. Feminist
hermeneutics has raised for us a new, critical
question: what was the world of experience of
women in biblical times? This is not a new
hermeneutic but a new question. Since the record
of revelation centered around males in the culture
in which it was received, no specific attention was
given to the consciousness of women in that culture. We have to go back to the texts and try to
find clues to this specific question. We also need
to examine non-biblical texts to try to find
information on the subject.

As we go back to the text we will find more and
more signs which point to the experience of women
in biblical times. When we take into account the
bias of the culture, the patriarchal structure of
the family, the eyes of the male writers, and other
such items that may have skewed the writing, we can
project, to some extent, what the experience of
women in that time was.

We need to correct as much as possible the
falsehoods that have crept into the text, the
translations, and the interpretations of Scripture.
This involves such items as:

—establishing again the original text (e.g. Rom. 16:7 should read Junia [female] and not Junias [male]).

--changing lectionaries and Bible dictionaries where these have given false information.

--retranslating, so as not to perpetuate a gender bias or a distortion that does not appear in the original text. (This applies especially to the use of "man" in the generic sense).

--seeking to arrive at more inclusive language in our theologizing and in our proclamation.

--working through our biblical and systematic theology on the basis of new understandings of women as reflected in Jesus and the early church but as rejected by the long history of interpretation of the Church.

A basic reworking requires concerted effort, diligence and much patience. Some changes will not be realized until the language we use gives us new possibilities of speech. These new inclusive words and phrases have to be coined and become standard usage before we will be totally free from the bondage of present language. We can suggest new words, phrases, and thought patterns which promise to be better than the present language forms, and if they are accepted and acted on by others, a change will have taken place. It is a task for the individual, the corporate church and the public at large. A new question, a new consciousness does create a new life and a new language. Here, too, we need to free (loose) ourselves from that which leads to death, and bind ourselves to that which leads to life.

# A HERMENEUTICAL CHALLENGE FOR WOMANISTS:
## THE INTERRELATION BETWEEN THE TEXT
## AND OUR EXPERIENCE

### Toinette M. Eugene

In the Pulitzer Prize winning novel, The Color
Purple, author Alice Walker has one of her principal characters insist to another central woman figure that she cannot even begin to imagine an image
of God for herself until she removes from the field
of her vision an androcentric version of the
Divine.

> Well, us talk and talk bout God, but I'm
> still adrift. Trying to chase that old
> white man out of my head....You have to get
> man off your eyeball, before you can see
> anything a'tall....He on your box of grits,
> in your head, and all over the
> radio....Whenever you trying to pray, and
> man plop himself on the other end of it,
> tell him to get lost, say Shug. Conjure up
> flowers, wind, water, a big rock.

This brief bit of dialogue indicates what is
for me a central concern in attempting to identify
the hermeneutical challenge for investigating
Scripture from a feminist perspective. This concern is that while we attempt to articulate a public and biblical theology of shalom here, we must
understand that we cannot reform sexism as something separate or unconnected to other oppressive
ideologies such as racism, militarism, or
imperialism. The structures of oppression are all
intrinsically linked; simply resolving the problems
of sexism in relation to Scriptural texts will in
no way make us whole.
Each of us brings to this discussion some pre-
understandings from our culture and conditioning.
These pre-understandings may serve as a foundation
for furthering our dialogue in relationship to the
contributions which feminist scholarship is making
to the enterprise of biblical hermeneutics. My own
pre-understandings are shaped by my identity as a
black Catholic woman trained in the disciplines of
theology and education. It is for this reason that
I want to indicate from the outset that although

collectively we may be focusing primarily on the
inherent obstacles of sexism, or on the predicament
posed by patriarchal texts, it is vital for me to
keep before all of us the principle derived from my
own pre-understandings: that all ideologies of
dominance and subordination are intrinsically
linked.

If we separate out and examine sexism for the
purposes of arriving at a more integrated biblical
theology of shalom, then we must understand, as
Alice Walker and other non-white feminists have so
astutely pointed out to us, that sexism is not a
single issue which can be dealt with as a isolated
entity, unconnected to anything else. For me, to
identify the hermeneutical challenge of Scripture
by seeking to articulate the interrelation between
the texts and my experience requires that the kind
of liberation theology which I express must be mul-
tidimensional in its reach and grasp.

The conversation which Shug and Celie have in
that brief portion from The Color Purple cited
above is paradigmatic of the points which I want to
present as my own premises. As these characters
struggle to know God, to be their own best selves
as women, and to act as liberated persons in the
pursuit of their own calling, what becomes apparent
is that the oppressions which they experience due
to race, sex, class, and caste must be transformed
together, not as separate problems which have some
isolated impact on their human condition. In this
context, I want to lay out for you some assumptions
which I hold about the nature of liberation
hermeneutics as it interacts with feminist theology. In this paradigmatic context which is
illustrative of the interrelation which I experience between the liberating texts of Scripture and
my experience, I submit that there is a new and
more praxis-oriented model of critical interpretation which is even now emerging.

## Insights of Liberationist Hermeneutics

Liberation theologians have worked out a distinctive approach to biblical interpretation that
leads to a redefinition of criteria for public
theological discourse. Instead of asking whether
an approach is appropriate to the Scriptures and
adequate to the human condition,[2] one first tests

to see whether a theological model of biblical
interpretation is <u>adequate</u> to the historical-
literary method of contemporary interpretation and
<u>appropriate</u> to the struggle of the oppressed for
liberation.

While it is to be understood that the hermeneu-
tic-contextual approach advocates the elimination
of all presuppositions and pre-understandings for
the sake of objective-descriptive exegesis, there
is an alternative methodology which stands in contrast to this approach, and which is more reflec-
tive of what I choose to call liberationist interpretation. Proceeding from an existential perspective, liberationist hermeneutics defines <u>pre-
understanding</u> as the common existential ground
between the interpreter and the author of the text.
Some political theologians have challenged this
choice of existential philosophy while liberation
theologians maintain a hermeneutics of engagement
instead of a hermeneutics of detachment. Since it
is obvious that no complete detachment or value-
neutrality is possible, according to this liberationist hermeneutic, the biblical interpreter must
make her or his stance explicit and then take an
advocacy position in favor of the oppressed. For
an authentic liberationist interpretation of the
Bible, it is necessary to acknowledge the hermeneutical privilege of the oppressed and to develop
a hermeneutics "from below."[3]

Theology is explicitly or implicitly inter-
twined with the existing social situation, according to contemporary liberation theologians. To
respond to this foundational assumption and claim,
the methodology of the hermeneutic circle is proposed as one means by which the oppressed are
enabled to examine social and sacred tradition or a
biblical text by means of a dialectic which is
oriented to establishing new and liberating interpretations and praxis for their situation.[4] The
hermeneutic circle begins with a way of experiencing and analyzing social reality that leads to
suspicion about the reasons for maintaining an
oppressive situation. At the second level of the
circle we apply our suspicion to theology as well
as to all other ideological institutions and
instructional realities in our lives. At a third
level there comes a new way of experiencing theo-

logical reality in particular, which in turn leads us to the more exegetical suspicion that "the prevailing interpretation of the Bible has not taken important pieces of data into account."[5]

At the last level we bring these insights to bear upon the interpretation of Scripture. Only active commitment to the oppressed and active involvement in their struggle for liberation enable us to see our society and our world differently and give us a new perspective for looking at the scriptural text in relation to our situation in the world. Thus, praxis for liberation evolving out of our new interpretation completes the hermeneutic circle and gives impetus and momentum for spiralling forward in faith and with a renewed consciousness.

## Insights of Feminist Hermeneutics

Feminist theology, in agreement with and in addition to Latin American and Black Liberation theologies, begins with a hermeneutics of suspicion that applies to both contemporary androcentric interpretations of the Bible and the biblical texts themselves. Like other liberation theologies, feminist theology begins with the experience—in this case, the experience of women. In our struggle for self-identity, survival, and liberation in a patriarchal church and society, Christian women have found that the Bible has been used as a weapon against us. But at the same time, it has been a resource for hope, courage, and commitment in the struggle. Therefore, it cannot be the task of feminist interpretation solely to defend the Bible against its feminist critics, but to understand and interpret it in such a way that both its oppressive and its liberative power are clearly recognized.

From its inception, feminist interpretation of Scripture has been generated by the fact that the Bible was used to halt the emancipation of women and slaves.[6] Reclaiming the Bible as a feminist heritage and resource is only possible because it has not functioned simply and exclusively to legitimate the oppression of all women: freeborn, slave, black and white, Native American, European and Asian, immigrant, poor, working class and middle class, Third World and First World women. It is overwhelmingly clear that the Scriptures have

also provided authorization and legitimization for
women who have rejected slavery, racism, anti-
semitism, colonial exploitation, and misogynism as
unbiblical and against God's will. The Bible has
inspired countless women to speak out and to struggle against our experiences of injustice, exploitation, and stereotyping. The biblical vision of
freedom and shalom still energizes women in all
walks of life and from entirely different cultural
conditions and pre-understandings to continue to
struggle against poverty, slavery, dehumanization,
and denigration.

A critical feminist hermeneutics of liberation
therefore seeks to develop a critical dialectical
mode of biblical interpretation that can do justice
to all women's experiences of the Bible as a
thoroughly patriarchal book written in androcentric
language as well as to women's liberating experience of the Bible as a source of empowerment and
vision in our struggles for liberation.

Such a hermeneutics has to subject biblical
texts to a dialectical process of critical readings
and feminist evaluations. In order to do so, feminist biblical interpretation must insist that the
litmus test for invoking Scripture as the Word of
God must be whether or not biblical texts and
traditions seek to end all relations based on
oppressive domination and exploitation. In short,
as Alice Walker, Jacquelyn Grant, Katie Cannon, and
others have said in relation to black women and
black theology (and which applies to a criterion
about all women and minorities in relation to
normative theology), if we claim that oppressive
patriarchal texts are the Word of God, then we
proclaim God as a God of oppression and dehumanization.

Feminist biblical hermeneutics is not simply a
theologically faddish methodology or perspective,
but it is emphatically a form of interpretation
that is at the core of women's liberation movement
in church and society. Similarly, patriarchal
oppression is not simply identical with androcentrism or sexism, and thus unconnected to other
oppressive ideologies. Patriarchy defines not just
women, but also subjugated peoples and races as
"the others" to be dominated. Women of color and
poor women are doubly and triply oppressed in such

a patriarchal social system.

A feminist biblical hermeneutics must remain an essential and critical component of any theology of liberation as long as women and other disenfranchised minorities suffer the injustice and oppression of patriarchal structures. This kind of liberation theology explores the particular experiences of women with others who are struggling for liberation from systemic patriarchy, and at the same time indicts all oppressive patriarchal structures and texts, especially those of biblical religion. Such a theology seeks to name the alienation, anger, pain, and dehumanization engendered by patriarchal sexism and racism in society and church. At the same time it seeks to articulate an alternative liberating vision and praxis for all oppressed people by utilizing the paradigm of women's experiences of survival and salvation in the struggle against patriarchal oppression and degradation.

To advocate the women's liberation movement in biblical religion as the hermeneutical center of a feminist critical theology of liberation[8] and to speak of the ekklesia of women[9] does not mean to advocate a separatist strategy. But it does mean that it is necessary to boldly underscore the visibility and experience of women in biblical religion and to safeguard their freedom within it and within related institutional churches from all oppressive androcentric control.

According to Elizabeth Schüssler Fiorenza, to make a systematically articulated feminist experience central to biblical interpretation and theological reflection requires a paradigm shift in biblical interpretation--a shift from understanding the Bible as archetypal myth to understanding it as historical prototype.[10] Moreover, I would argue that it concomitantly requires a paradigmatic shift in the way we understand ourselves as self-conscious and moral human beings who are shaped by and therefore capable of creatively interpreting the Word of God which has been freely and indiscriminately offered to all people in Christ.

A Hermeneutical Challenge for Womanists

In the introduction to In Search of Our
Mother's Gardens, Alice Walker proposes the descriptive term, "womanist" as a word which (although
it refers primarily to a black feminist) is derived
from a term for those whose behavior is most often
audacious, outrageous, or in brief, iconoclastic to
say the very least.[11] She further describes a
womanist as one "who loves the Spirit, loves struggle, loves the [common] folk, loves self. Regard-
less."[12] It is possible for us to understand ourselves as 'womanists' doing biblical hermeneutics
in this context. However, it would mean then,
according to Walker, that we would be committed to
espousing alternative standards of a lifestyle and
a methodology which are most certainly to be experienced as contradictory or paradoxical to those of
the dominant society. Nonetheless, the practical
implications of choosing to participate in such a
paradigm shift still offer encouragement for me.

If the hermeneutical challenge is to be found
in making the connections between the text and our
experience, then I believe that as we critically
engage in a dialectic which acknowledges and
respects even the most diverse and seemingly dis-
tant identities and pre-understandings which exist
among us, we shall have the opportunity to articulate and to experience a new form of biblical
shalom. In the act of investing ourselves in the
praxis of this entirely new model of critical
interpretation, we may become recipients as well as
co-creators of the peace that is consonant with our
historical beginnings and with our ultimate
eschatological longing for God.

## Notes

1. Alice Walker, The Color Purple (New York: Harcourt Brace Jovanovich, 1982), 168.

2. See Adrienne Rich, "Toward a Woman-Centered University" in Florence Howe, ed., Women and the Power to Change (NY: McGraw Hill, 1975), 15-46; Elizabeth Schüssler Fiorenza, "Toward a Liberating and Liberated Theology: Women Theologians and Feminist Theology in the U.S.A.," Concilium 115 (1979), 22-23.

3. See Lee Cormie, "The Hermeneutical Privilege of the Oppressed: Liberation Theologies, Biblical Faith, and Marxist Sociology of Knowledge," Proceedings of the Catholic Theological Society of America 32 (1978), 155-181.

4. This whole section is based on an analysis of Juan Luis Segundo, The Liberation of Theology (Maryknoll: Orbis Press, 1976).

5. Juan Luis Segundo, 33ff.

6. Willard Swartley, Slavery, Sabbath, War and Women: Case Studies in Biblical Interpretation (Scottdale, PA: Herald Press, 1983).

7. Jacquelyn Grant, "Black Theology and the Black Woman," in G. S. Wilmore and J. H. Cone, eds., Black Theology: A Documentary History: 1966-79 (Maryknoll: Orbis Press, 1979), 418-433; "A Black Response to Feminist Theology," in J. Kalven and M. I. Buckley eds., Women's Spirit Bonding (New York: Pilgrim Press, 1984), 117-124.

Katie Cannon, "The Emergence of Black Feminist Consciousness," in Letty Russell, ed., Feminist Interpretation of the Bible (Philadelphia: Westminster Press, 1985), 30-40; "Resources for a Constructive Ethic in the Life and Work of Zora Neale Hurston," Journal of Feminist Studies in Religion 1 (Spring, 1985) 37-51.

See in particular the contribution of Katie Cannon in the Mudflower Collective, God's Fierce Whimsy: Christian Feminism and Theological Education (New York: Pilgrim Press, 1985).

8. Rosemary Radford Ruether, Sexism and God Talk: Toward a Feminist Theology (Boston: Beacon Press, 1983).

9. Elizabeth Schüssler Fiorenza, In Memory of Her: A Feminist Theological Reconstruction of Christian Origins (New York: Crossroad Press, 1984).

10. Elizabeth Schüssler Fiorenza, _Bread Not Stone: The Challenge of Feminist Biblical Interpretation_ (Boston: Beacon Press, 1984), 15.

11. Alice Walker, _In Search of Our Mother's Gardens: Womanist Prose_ (Harcourt Brace Jovanovich, 1983) xi-xii.

12. Ibid.

# MODERN WOMEN AND ANCIENT WRITING:
## A TENSIVE LITERARY MODEL FOR FEMINIST HERMENEUTICS

Mary Schertz

A great deal of the contemporary feminist interpretation of ancient texts, whether the Jewish and Christian scriptures or texts representing other ancient traditions, relies upon a method that can perhaps be best described as allegorical. With varying degrees of sophistication, these writers assume that the female characters in the text under scrutiny "stand for" what happened to women in history while the male characters "stand for" what men did to women in history. The text is then interpreted in light of this external framework. While the method is most clearly discernable in narrative materials, where allegory operates in a relationship of natural attraction, it is also discernable in the interpretation of other kinds of material. In dealing with a didactic text such as the epistle to the Ephesians, for instance, feminist interpretation typically reconstructs a dramatic setting in which the letter functions as a "speech" by one of the characters in a "play." These characters are then allegorized in much the same way as the characters in the ancient narratives are allegorized. Albeit one step removed from the text, the method remains essentially the same.

The prevalence of this mode can be readily discerned in the work of some of the most prominent feminist scholars in religion. Mary Daly views the NT depiction of Mary as a representation of the "tamed Goddess."[1] Rosemary Radford Ruether describes the Genesis account of the creation of Eve from Adam's body as portraying "precisely this situation of the male reborn into the male-identified world, where the woman is given to him as auxiliary to his male identity."[2] Elizabeth Schüssler Fiorenza essentially sees the NT corpus as representing different voices in a "process of gradual ecclesial patriarchalization which entails the historically necessary development. . . from the egalitarian charismatic structures of the beginning to the hierarchical order of the Constantinian church."[3] As is evident even in these small samples, each of these scholars has her own interests and positions. Yet, interestingly

enough, each interprets texts by referencing them
to an historical construct external to the text.

In making these observations, I am not suggesting that the work of these interpreters is bad
because they work in the mode of historical
allegory. After all, this mode has proven itself
to be a powerful interpretive tool down through the
ages. More precisely, the mode has produced significant results. The consequence of these and
other studies is an unquestionably clearer understanding of the dynamics of women's oppression
through the centuries. All of us, of whatever per-
suasion, are greatly indebted to the ground-
breaking work of these and other feminist scholars.

I am suggesting, however, that a particular and
somewhat limited concept of the power and authority
of texts lurks beneath this mode and that the
limitations of the concept confuse the goals of
feminist interpretation in a specific way. That
confusion indicates that feminist interpretation
might benefit from exploration of additional
options with respect to both the view of textual
power/authority and to the modes of interpretation
available to feminist scholars. In this essay I
want to suggest a model for feminist hermeneutics
that is grounded in an alternative view of textual
authority. Then, I want to use the issues of
authority, both textual authority and the authority
of women's experience, to focus the development of
the model itself.

## I.  Textual Authority--Alternative Views

The kind of power Daly, Ruether and Fiorenza
give to the texts they are interpreting by means of
historical allegorization is the kind of power one
grants a text which one believes to represent,
albeit partially and/or covertly, "what really happened." The real distinctions between their interpretation of Hebrew and Christian scriptures, for
example, and the interpretations of fundamentalist
Christians are disagreements as to: 1) whether the
texts represent what actually happened covertly or
overtly, partially or fully; 2) disagreements about
how those happenings are to be evaluated. Granted
that there are broad variations in both camps as to
how well these points are argued, one still concludes that, in both cases, the text is viewed as

possessing the power to represent what actually
happened.

While one could criticize this particular view
on a variety of grounds--its affinity to a kind of
positivism that modern feminism has generally
rejected, for instance--I am critical of this view
because it confuses what I am calling a first, second and third order critical process. There seems
to me to be three kinds of critical processes
appropriate to feminist interpretation. The first
is, or should be, operative in the detailed
"exegesis" of the text. The topic of concern is
how a particular woman's experience, that of the
interpreter, interacts with the text she is interpreting. The question of whether the text
oppresses/liberates women is not absent, but it is
necessarily individualized and it is but one of
many questions brought to the text by the interpreter.

The second order critical process is, or should
be, operative in a somewhat broader context--the
community of feminist textual scholars. The concern is how women's experience in general interacts
with the text. This process is constituted by
inter-subjective debate as feminist scholars compare and evaluate the alternative readings proposed
by feminist individuals. The question of whether
the text oppresses/liberates women is an important
question at this point, but the main concern is
what constitutes a good reading of the text from a
feminist perspective.

The third order critical process is, or should
be, operative in a variety of contexts that are
broader than the community of feminist scholars
and, at the same time, more localized. These contexts are broader in that the debates--whether con-
ducted in congregations, particular communities of
women, various liberation/political movements,
etc.--include people with other disciplinary and
vocational perspectives. The contexts are more
narrow in that the debates are necessarily focused
and shaped by each particular group's purposes and
needs. The question of whether the text oppresses/
liberates women is one of the main topics of concern in these debates. While the first and second
order critical processes are primary resources for
these communal debates, feminist scholars individu-

ally and collectively must accept the fact that the
question  of whether and how texts oppress/liberate
women  is a properly communal concern and that different  groups working with the same data,, in different contexts may reach different conclusions.

The  problem  with  the  mode  of  historical
allegorization  is  that it tends to collapse these
discrete  processes.  Because the mode consists of
relating  elements  of  the  text to elements of an
historical construct which, in the case of feminist
hermeneutics,  dramatizes  the domination of women,
the larger questions of how the text interacts with
women's  experience in general (i.e. does this text
oppress  women?)  automatically  become  dominant in
the  consideration.  The main interpretive interaction  takes  place  between the interpreter and the
historical context because the most important decisions  are whether and how elements in the text fit
the  construct.  The properly private interaction
between  the  interpreter  and the text as text (or
first  order critical process) is aborted while the
properly public interactions (the debate among feminist  scholars  and  the  communal  assessment  of
whether  the  text  oppresses/liberates  women) are
absorbed into the private.

The  construct  of  the  power of a text as the
capacity to represent history is, however, only one
construct  of  textual  power.  An alternative to a
view  of  a  text  as having the power to represent
what  really  happened  is  the view of a text--any
text  whether  "sacred" or otherwise--as having the
power  to  communicate a message. Susan Sniader
Lanser  describes this view of textual authority as
follows:

> The  term  'author' designates not only the
> producer(s)  of  a  message,  but a special
> kind  of  formalized power--authority--which
> the  sender  has (presumably) received from
> the  relevant  social  community. . . The
> verbal  act,  in  other  words, implies not
> only  a  sender, receiver, and message, but
> some  potential  for  successful  speech
> activity  which depends for its realization
> on  the  sender's  authority  and  the [4]
> receiver's validation of this authority.

If we move from granting a text authority on the basis of its representation of what happened, to granting a text the authority consonant with its illocutionary force, we have effectively broken the issue of textual authority into a variety of options. Instead of the stark either/or (either the authority of the text or the authority of women's experience) posited by Daly and, increasingly, by Ruether, we are free to grant different kinds of textual authority to different kinds of texts. The authority granted will be correlated both to the text's establishment of its own authority for its own purposes and also to the interpreter's validation or non-validation of this authority at the level of a first order critical process. My contention is that feminist principles (principles forged, in part, by feminist scholars operating in the allegorical mode) can be useful in both parts of this operation.

While these interpretive steps do not directly answer the big questions of whether the Hebrew and Christian scriptures oppress or liberate women, they do make several contributions to that debate. Utilization of the model should give greater emphasis to the private process between the interpreter and the text and thereby encourage interpretations which take seriously both the authority of the texts as written and the authority of particular women's experience. The sheer production of such interpretations should facilitate greater precision in qualitative assessments. In other words, utilization of the model should assist in an effort to begin setting up some criteria as to what constitutes good feminist readings of texts. Greater strength at the level of the first and second order critical processes should, at some point, contribute to a renewed communal effort to consider those questions of which texts are authoritative for women, an effort that will be characterized by both care for good reading and justice for women. If our aim, as feminist textual scholars, is to vitalize this process, the critical need would appear to be the expansion of our options at the operation of the first order critical process. The proposed model is one attempt at such expansion.

## II.  An Interpretive Model

The interpretive model consonant with a view of
the power of texts as the power to communicate a
message is a model based on an activity of written
communication--reception of a written message, or,
in other words, reading. This model of interpretation will be developed here with the assistance of
four theorists--two of whom are literary theorists
and two of whom are feminist hermeneuts. We will
look first to Wayne C. Booth for a basic description of how textual authority functions. Secondly,
we will use hermeneutical principles developed by
Elizabeth Schüssler Fiorenza to articulate the
critique of Booth's model consonant with feminist
ideology and to establish a basic understanding of
how the authority of women's experience functions
in interpretation. Thirdly, we will turn to
Wolfgang Iser to assist in a mediation between the
two poles of textual authority and the authority of
women's experience. The effort at this point is
not to resolve the tension but to transform it from
dysfunctional to functional tension. Finally,
Janice Capel Anderson will provide some practical
assistance on ways to create meaningful interpretation from the cauldron of the tension.

## Textual Authority

In granting a text the authority correlative to
its illocutionary purpose, we are saying[6] little
more than that if a text is worth reading, it is
worth understanding. In this respect, the investment of authority is an act of adopting the role of
"implied" or "ideal" reader within the acknowledged
limitations of our actual status as real readers.
While there are a number of formulations of this
relationship, one of the more helpful outlines is
provided by Wayne C. Booth. Some of Booth's
definitions are obviously more suited to the study
of modern literature, which contains far more com-
plexity than the texts with which we are primarily
concerned. Nevertheless, several parts of his construction of the varieties of readers can be helpful to our task. For instance, Booth characterizes
the real reader as someone who is willing to be a
"working listener," someone who responds to "seemingly inert" signs in a text. Secondly, this working listener should not only respond to the signs

of the text, but be the "kind of reader selected, or implied, by a given tale." This reader's knowledge and values coincide with the knowledge and values set forth in the text--even though the actual knowledge and values of the "flesh and blood" reader may differ considerably from those of the reader constructed or posited by the text. Thirdly, this reader is not only a working listener and the reader selected or implied by the text, but also one who "joins the implied author in creating an 'improved version' of the self."[7] In other words, the reader is someone who will allow himself or herself to be changed and shaped by the text.

While Booth is by no means so naive as to intimate that this "ideal" relationship can be achieved in any complete sense, he is quite clear that accurate reception of the message involves a certain intellectual attitude on the part of the reader, a willingness to be influenced by the text. Without this willingness, the text cannot be actualized, it cannot fulfill its intent, it cannot be understood. Unless we are willing to acknowledge that at some level we do not understand the texts which we are interpreting, we must come to texts with some degree of openness to their influence over us. Granting a text the authority of its illocutionary purpose is required for understanding its message.

## The Authority of Women's Experience
While Booth's depiction of the implied or ideal reader has a wonderfully "genteel sensibility" about it, the concept cannot escape the brunt of the feminist critique. The obvious problem is the fact that adopting, even temporarily, the role of implied reader is to submit, even temporarily, to the knowledge and values of texts that are certainly patriarchal and frequently misogynist. After all, Fiorenza has staged the kind of comprehensive examination of a thorough-going androcentrism in the ancient texts that few if any feminists would want to deny. She has not only described this androcentrism, but she has convincingly argued against both the possibility and the desirability of relinquishing one's "theoretical presuppositions and political allegiances"[8] in the act of interpretation. Moreover, she advocates a

act of interpretation.[8] Moreover, she advocates a
hermeneutical method that boldly claims the
allegiances of feminist liberation movements as an
authoritative corrective to the androcentrism of
the texts and invites women to activate their experience in the praxis of reconstruction.

At this point, Booth's sympathetic implied
reader and Fiorenza's suspicious feminist hermeneut
would appear to be diametrically opposed.
Seemingly, we must choose between the authority of
the text and the authority of women's experience.

## Interpreting Within the Tension

Insoluble as the dilemma may appear, the work
of Wolfgang Iser is helpful in working through the
tensions between these conflicting authorities--
not, as mentioned earlier, to the point where the
tensions are resolved, but to the point where they
become functional rather than dysfunctional. Iser
actualizes the tension, or sets the tension in
motion by positing the two poles that we have set
up as the authority of the text and the authority
of women's experience. (The fact that he uses different vocabulary does not hinder the application
and we will remain with the categories we have
established in this essay for the sake of
simplicity.) Having established these two poles,
he concludes that "the work itself" is not identical with either pole but takes place "somewhere
between the two." He says that "as the reader
passes through the various perspectives offered by
the text and relates the different views and patterns to one another he sets the work in motion,[9]
and so sets himself in motion too."

The shift of the work from the text itself to
the interaction between the text and the reader is
a significant shift for feminist hermeneutics.
What Iser is saying means we do not need to let the
texts have "authority over" us in order to understand the message. Being the "working listener"
that Booth formulates means being sensitive to the
clues provided in the text but it does not mean
passivity on the part of the reader nor does it
mean she has to suspend her feminist persuasions.
Rather she participates in the creation of the message, she "'receives' it by composing it."[10] In
fact, this model precludes the suspension of one's

and values would "entail the loss of the tension
which is a precondition for the processing and the
comprehension that follows it."[11] Thus Iser provides a way for feminist hermeneuts to "have it
both ways"--to be good readers and to maintain the
energy and spirit of their commitment to the liberation of women. Indeed, for feminists as for
everyone else, interpretation "happens" in the
tensive relationship of these multiple commit-
ments--commitments that include the compulsion
toward understanding the text and the compulsion
toward the growth and freedom of women.

## Gender Reading
    Having established some notion that the tension
between the authority of texts and the authority of
women's experience is not an unconquerable obstacle
but a possibility for the creation of meaning, we
are in a position to speculate what specific
insights a feminist orientation might contribute to
this interpretive construct. Iser does not provide
much assistance in such practical matters and, in
light of the relatively recent advent of any kind
of feminist interpretation, we might conclude that
such insights are yet to be discovered. However
Janice Capel Anderson, in her work with the Gospel
of Matthew, has at least suggested some possibilities we might want to consider.
    In the first part of her article Anderson des-
cribes how the experience of a feminist hermeneut
resonates with specific gender issues in the book
of Matthew. While this aspect is an important part
of the task before us, the model being proposed
purports to be useful for texts that do not contain
specific gender content as well as for those which
do. In other words, the issues of feminist interpretation include but extend beyond texts in which
women play a role as characters, addressees or
authors.
    It is this larger concern which Anderson
addresses in the second part of the article. She
concludes that, by adopting the role of the implied
reader, the feminist hermeneut responds for herself
to an invitation issued by the text. This invitation is to "stand with" the narrator who, in turn,
"stands with" the character Jesus in his evaluation
of the story world. Jesus' evaluation of this

world is an evaluation in which "wealth, occupa-
tion, purity, ethnicity, and family ties are less
important than the stance characters take in relationship to Jesus." Thus, adopting the role of the
implied reader or, in the terms of this essay,
granting the illocutionary authority of the text,
frees feminist readers "to judge the ideological
stances of the various character groups, male and
female. In following the guidance of the narrator
and Jesus, the actual reader may also be led to
judge some of the patriarchal assumptions implicit
in their ideological view points."[12]

Clearly, Anderson points the way for feminist
readers to do more than simply add "a woman's perspective" to the dozens of readings available on
any biblical text. There would seem to be room in
this model for deconstructing certain patriarchal
elements in certain texts. The model does not, of
course, permit careless deconstruction. That
interpretive function, too, must be accountable to
the illocutionary authority of the text. What
works for Anderson in relation to Matthew may or
may not work for other feminist interpreters in
relation to other texts. Anderson's exegesis is
but one example of how the model may be useful in
the tasks of interpretation. But, I suggest, additional exploration of the model may be worth some
effort. The model does allow feminists to let the
authority of their own experience stand alongside
the authority of texts. It may allow more of us to
live more creatively with more texts. It may allow
us to swim in our historical/textual stream and to
trouble its waters with our feminist outrage.

## Notes

1. Mary  Daly, Pure Lust:  Elemental Feminist
Philosophy (Boston:   Beacon Press, 1984), 92.
2. Rosemary  Radford Ruether,  Womanguides:
Readings  Toward a Feminist Theology (Boston:  Beacon Press, 1985), 63.
3. Elizabeth  Schüssler Fiorenza, In Memory of
Her: A Feminist Theological Reconstruction of
Christian Origins (New York:  Crossroad, 1983), 80.
4. Susan  Sniader  Lanser,  The Narrative Act:
Point  of  View in Prose Fiction (Princeton:   Princeton University Press, 1981), 80.
5. Speech act theory describes any act of communication  as having three aspects.  The locution-
ary  aspect  has to do with the content of the message  itself.  The perlocutionary aspect has to do
with the effect the message has on the recipient of
the  message.  The illocutionary aspect has to do
with  how the message is delivered--for example, as
a  threat,  a  promise,  a  command,  a  wish, etc.
Lanser  acknowledges her indebtedness to speech act
theory  throughout her book, but see especially pp.
62, 63.
6. I am  neither actually raising nor totally
ignoring  the  issues  of why a particular feminist
interpreter  is  dealing with  a  particular text.
This  choice  is,  of  course, guided by factors of
both  personal  interest and external authorities--
whether  ecclesial, academic, cultural etc. The
issues  of  the  power  exercised  in  the  initial
encounter between text and reader are appropriately
pertinent  to  feminist  discussion but are,  for
reasons of time and space, assumed rather than ana-
lyzed in this essay.
7. Wayne  C.  Booth,  The Rhetoric of Fiction,
Second  Edition (Chicago:   University of Chicago
Press, 1983), 428-29.
8. Fiorenza,  xvii as well as elsewhere.  This
tenet is basic to her construct.
9. Wolfgang  Iser, The Act of Reading: A
Theory  of  Aesthetic  Response (Baltimore:  Johns
Hopkins University Press, 1978), 21.
10. Ibid.
11. Ibid., p. 37.
12. Janice  Capel  Anderson, "Matthew:  Gender
and Reading," Semeia (1983), 23.

# THE HERMENEUTICAL CHALLENGE

Diane L. MacDonald

Hermeneutics is at heart a search for critical principles in a world thoroughly historical. No interpretation escapes historical conditioning. No perspective can be absolutized. Yet if we are to avoid nihilism, we must make judgments. We must distinguish between better and worse interpretations and have a basis for doing so. What then is the basis for critical judgment in our historical world?

Hans-Georg Gadamer in Truth and Method has pioneered a pathway through the maze of possible solutions. Central to his proposal of a "fusion of horizons" is a critique of both the Enlightenment's "objectivism" and the ensuing Romantic swing to "subjectivism." The objectivist claims that there is one true interpretation of text. The interpreter, by ridding her/himself of all bias, uncovers the truth. In contrast, the subjectivist claims that all humans share a psychological substratum which allows for understanding to take place across the gulfs of time and place. The interpreter, in this view, has access to the mind of an author based on their common humanity. Here empathy is the key to true interpretation. In spite of these differences between the "objectivist" and the "subjectivist," both rely on a Cartesian subject/object split which has been a barrier to true understanding by perpetuating structures of domination.

Gadamer's "fusion of horizons" is neither "objectivist" nor "subjectivist." It is inter-subjective. That is, it recognizes a dynamic between text and interpreter that is mutually influential. The interpreter is influenced by the text: the text, in turn, is seen anew, and gains new meaning through the reading of the interpreter. Neither is static and univocal.

Two reasons given by Gadamer for the productive dynamic between text and interpreter are (1) "positive prejudice" and (2) the "effective history" of texts. Prejudice, counter to the claims of the Enlightenment, is not necessarily closed and reductionistic. It can be a helpful, orienting predisposition to new, enlarged understanding. Likewise, the meaning is its "effective history"--its function within its original

social setting along with its rich and multiple history of functions in various settings throughout its
usage in a religious tradition.

In approaching a text, an interpreter, conscious
of her own historical situatedness, dialogues with the
text in an effort to expand her understanding. As she
examines the way in which this text functioned within
its original setting as well as the way it has functioned throughout the history of its usage, she
becomes more aware of its limitations and possibilities for her situation. To the extent that the
text "speaks to her," that is, grips her imagination
and feeds or expands her own world construct, this
text is true. To the extent that the text is rote,
dull, unintelligible or defiant of her construct, it
holds no truth for her.

Attention therefore must be given the "prejudices"
or "world constructs" with which the interpreter
approaches a text. Contrary to a "subjectivist" perspective which sees prejudice (sometimes called
"preunderstanding") as a privatistic orientation, subject to the whims of an individual, for Gadamer
prejudice is a deeply embedded social construction of
reality shaped by one's culture and tradition yet mal-
leable to the individual's actions and decisions. As
explicated more fully by Clifford Geertz, these social
constructs are a complex of symbols fed by particular
cultural, linguistic, and religious symbolic worlds
within which an orienting ethic operates. Critical to
the task of understanding—whether of texts or more
present "subjects"—is a growing self-consciousness of
one's social construction of reality and attendant
critical reflection on the adequacy of its operant
orienting ethic.

Interpretation, in this view, is a dynamic between
two horizons—that of the text and that of the interpreter. The horizons of meaning of the text arise out
of its social function within its original context
along with its history of usage in the tradition. The
horizons of meaning of the interpreter arise out of
the interpreter's social construction of reality—her
symbolic "world construct."

In the dynamic of text and interpreter, not all
conversation culminates in a "fusion of horizons." At
times, the horizons of meaning of the text are too
strange or unintelligible to the interpreter. At
times, the meanings are intelligible but go against

the grain of one's orienting ethic. Also, at times,
the interpreter's "world construct" is closed and
resistant to the possibilities of the text. Yet true
understanding, in Gadamer's terms, a "fusion of
horizons," can occur when the possibilities of a text
and the symbolic vision of the interpreter cohere.
And at such a time "truth" as new, enlarged understanding emerges.

What then does this perspective bring to a conversation among Mennonites on women and the Bible?
Because deconstruction nearly always precedes a helpful reconstruction, we begin with critique. What is
invalidated in a perspective that recognizes truth as
inter-subjective and open-ended?

For much of Mennonite history, the Bible has been
used as a sourcebook for univocal truth. While Mennonites may have avoided some of the more flagrant
abuses of positivism, they have habitually interacted
with the biblical text as if "truth" were encased in
its pages and "objectivity" were the key for unlocking
it. A problem, of course, arises when the Bible is
used to sanction discrimination against certain seg-
ments of our society, notably women, people of color,
and homosexuals. In the emerging recognition of such
discrimination, the first impulse of empathetic Mennonite scholars is to return to the text for a critique of these injustices and for validation of a more
egalitarian ethic. Differing from traditional Mennonites in predisposition, yet like them in method,
these scholars labor long and hard for the "true meaning" of the text. Not surprisingly, given their
laudable thirst for equality and justice, they fail to
find a biblical passage that contradicts their
predisposing orientation. Whether it is metaphors
like father, king, warrior, and lord, or household
injunctions like "Women, obey your husbands" or
"Slaves, obey your masters" all, they claim, support
inclusiveness and egalitarianism.

In a Gadamerian perspective, this drive for confirming our basic convictions by appeal to the "truth"
of the text is ultimately useless. The text does not
have one true meaning:    it has an "effective history"--a history of influence within many social settings. While the horizons of meaning within its
original context are important, they are neither
univocal nor normative. In this instance, in their
original social settings as well as in their histories

of influence, the biblical writings support both
sexism and equalitarianism depending upon the dynamic
between the text and the "world constructs" of its
varied readers.   By our repeated attempts to locate
our "truths" in the biblical texts--whether our
"truths" be sexist or egalitarian--we are avoiding
responsibility for our basic convictions and orienting
ethic.

Implicit in Gadamer's caution against locating
truth in a text is the inability of authors writing
many centuries ago to anticipate and resolve the
demands of our day.   Aside from our emerging consciousness of the historically intransigent domination
of men over the lives of women, we are beginning to
perceive other forms of domination which profoundly
threaten the life and future of the human community.
The economic stranglehold of first-world nations on
the third world has bled the people of underdeveloped
lands for centuries and been the breeding ground of
violent revolutions.  The greed of first-world peoples
for an accustomed high standard of living at the
expense of others--both within its boundaries and
without--has fed paranoia and an inflated defense
budget.   Given the dramatic escalation of nuclear
weapons and the parallel rise of cold-war slogan-
slinging, a nuclear holocaust looms large on the
horizon.   The problems of sexism, racism, militarism,
homophobia, and nationalism are subtly interconnected
in a complex of decisions and events that pose the
greatest threat to human existence ever encountered.

The answers are not located in the past--whether
it be the Bible for Christians or the Bagavahd Gita
for Hindus or the Torah for Jews or the Koran for Mus-
lims.   While these writings are immensely important
for providing paradigmatic symbols and stories within
their respective traditions, they cannot in themselves
be expected to provide tidy solutions to these contemporary threats.   We must take responsibility for
perceiving the ways in which our sacred texts have
perpetuated forms of domination and abuse, and critique them in light of contemporary experience.
Likewise, in our envisioning of what a global community might be, we are motivated and nourished by
those powerful symbols and stories of our respective
religious traditions which support human dignity and
equality.

Returning, then, to the specific question of women
and the Bible, an objectivist stance to the biblical

writings that tries to uncover the truth of equality
in every text is both inadequate and shortsighted. It
is inadequate because the biblical writings in themselves cannot adequately critique the patriarchal
structures of their own social settings and unequivo-
cally support an egalitarian ethic. To the extent
that biblical metaphors and stories perpetuate male
structures of domination over women, they are simply
not true for us. If we persist in this direction, if
we insist on confirming our orienting ethic by the
biblical text, we might win a few battles against
explicit forms of sexism in Mennonite churches (e.g.,
we might place a few women seminarians as pastors) but
we will lose the war against more insidious forms of
sexism as well as other forms of oppression also ens-
conced within our faith community.

An objectivist stance of interpretation is shortsighted because racism, militarism, homophobia, and
nationalism must be opposed as well. Instead of
squeezing the biblical texts for an "adequately"
respectful view of women's leadership in the church,
we should be using this challenge to reappraise and
readjust our basic orienting ethic that will in turn
inform our reading of the Bible. If Gadamer is correct that the criteria for receptivity and evaluation
of a text are not external to the interpretive process
and that we cannot get outside of our historicity for
normative judgments, then the hermeneutical challenge
of discerning criteria for evaluation within the
dynamic of text and interpreter necessitates giving
attention to our world constructs and orienting ethic.
To this we now turn.

One theologian within the Mennonite community who
even more than Gadamer recognizes the significance of
these social constructions of reality and the challenges of a world heading for self-destruction is Gordon D. Kaufman. In his books The Theological Imagination and Theology for a Nuclear Age, Kaufman offers a
way of re-examining our constructs through a series of
decisions in respect to the paradigmatic symbols of
God and Christ. This process is bipolar--examining on
the one hand the central issues of human historical
existence and, on the other, the functions of the
formative symbols of the Christian tradition. Kaufman's arguments for humanization as a goal and his
vision of God as a mysterious power propelling movement toward that goal are both credible and engaging.

His work is an especially important resource for us as
we  struggle  to reshape our goals and commitments and
reappropriate   our  religious  tradition  toward  the
redemption of the earth.

Only  through this difficult process of uncovering
our  orienting  ethic  and exposing it to the light of
broader  experiences and questions will we be equipped
to  return to the conversation with the biblical texts
for  deepening  of  the  vision  and  empowerment  for
action.   If  this is the direction in which our consultation on women and the Bible takes us, it will not
only  open some institutional doors for a few, it will
in  addition  create  new  doors of understanding that
will  better prepare us for the spectrum of challenges
that  affect  all  our  future, indeed the fate of the
earth.

Sources

Gadamer,  Hans-Georg.  Truth and Method (New York:
Seabury Press, 1975).

Geertz, Clifford.  The Interpretation of Cultures:
Selected Essays (New York:  Basic Books, 1973).

Kaufman,  Gordon  D.  The Theological Imagination:
Constructing  the Concept of God (Philadelphia:  Westminster Press, 1981).

_____.  Theology for a Nuclear Age (Philadelphia:
Westminster Press, 1985).

GOSHEN COLLEGE LIBRARY
GOSHEN, INDIANA

# HERMENEUTIC COMMUNITY--A FEMINIST CHALLENGE

## Lydia Harder

Central to the way Anabaptist/Mennonites have expressed their approach to Scripture interpretation has been an emphasis on the faith community as a hermeneutic community.[1] This stress on congregational interpretation was a way of saying that the relevatory truth of the biblical text could most readily be discerned within the context of a disciple community committed to following the Lord of Scripture. All members of the covenant community were to be responsible to participate in the process of determining the meaning of the Bible. Not the state, nor specialized theologians, nor hierarchical authorities were to be the final judge of the Bible's meaning. Rather accountability was to the whole community of faithful followers of Jesus. A process of dialogue and mutual counsel was to enable a congregation to live out the practical implications of the gospel message. Faith experience (salvation) was thus closely linked to faith knowledge (revelation). Instead of a sole emphasis on the objective revelation of the past, there was a shift to include the present faith experience as important in the process of hearing the dynamic Word of God in the Bible.

Feminist theology in common with other strands of liberation theology also contends that biblical interpretation must arise out of concrete communities.[2] Feminists understand these to be communities of liberation where women and men, struggling for equality and mutuality, become "prisms through which God's action in the mending of creation is to be understood."[3] They insist that communities whose praxis is liberating for all its members can more readily discern the meaning of Scripture. They agree that theology is not the exclusive prerogative of a select group of people--educated, trained, ordained men--but rather is the province of all persons. They point out that the oppressed who have experienced the grace of God in their new-found liberation and freedom have a particular contribution to make. The emphasis for feminists therefore is on defining more concretely the community best able to interpret the Bible.

46

Both Anabaptist/Mennonite hermeneutics and feminist hermeneutics acknowledge two poles in the interpretive process. They recognize that in the dialectical movement of Scripture interpretation both past revelatory knowledge and present faith experience are important. However feminist theology with its strong emphasis on salvation and liberation for all persons presents a particular challenge to Mennonites to spell out more clearly the shape of the hermeneutic community. As the definition of salvation is enlarged and adjusted to include the experience of women, the particular limitations and strengths of a specific hermeneutic community will be evident.

This paper will therefore focus on the shape of the hermeneutic community:  its tradition, its institutions and structures, and its language. The description of the importance of each of these aspects of community in the interpretive process is taken from recent philosophical theory. Specific critique comes from various feminist theologians.

1.  Communal tradition

Hans Georg Gadamer, one of the most important theoreticians of philosophical hermeneutics at the present time, has redefined the role of tradition in the hermeneutic process.[4] He understands tradition to be the historically formed pre-understanding with which an interpreter approaches a text.  Tradition is not something over against us but something in which we stand and within which things are perceived and defined. Thus both the context (horizon) of the interpreter and the context (horizon) of the text are involved in a dialectic process of interaction. Understanding takes place when a "fusion of horizons" occurs, when past and present come together to form the meaning of the text. The particular pre-judgments with which interpreters approach the text arise out of the tradition of the community of which they are a part.

Tradition, however, is not static, but dynamic and in motion, changing and moving in the encounter with the text. Unfruitful pre-judgments are discarded, and positive orientations are affirmed and enlarged as horizons interact and fuse. In this dialogical process there is always a partial nega-

tion of one's horizon (that is the tradition in
which we stand) in order to allow oneself to be
questioned by the text as well as to question.
Tradition must therefore be brought to consciousness and critically evaluated in order that new
insights from the text can emerge.

Church history and tradition have been of central concern to feminists, for they have realized
how important they are in providing the orientation
with which biblical interpreters approach their
task.    Feminists have argued that women were shut
out of the hermeneutic community for most of the
history of biblical interpretation. The foundational tradition arose out of male experience and
interaction with the text.    As Rosemary Ruether
points out, by not allowing women to study, teach
or preach, women have not only been excluded from
"shaping and interpreting the tradition from their
own experience, but the tradition has been shaped
and interpreted against them."[5]

As women begin to bring their experiences of
liberation and freedom in Christ to bear in the
dialogue with the text, a critical force is
unleashed which questions many traditional assumptions. The limitations of past formulations of the
meaning of the Jesus event are clearly seen when
female experiences of bondage and liberation are
taken seriously. A new inspiration is given for a
reconstruction of history where research focuses
particularly on the marginalized and forgotten
women in Christian history.[6]

Feminist theology thus presents a clear challenge to hermeneutic communities to evaluate and
test the tradition which informs their biblical
interpretation.    Have the presuppositions arisen
out of a tradition which took women's experiences
of God seriously? Are they being tested by women's
experiences of today? Communal tradition will not
stay untouched when women are fully included in the
hermeneutic community.

## 2.  Communal structures and institutions

The concepts of critical social philosophy
focus on a second aspect of the hermeneutic
community--the crucial communication process
between members of the community. It has become
increasingly evident that the discovery and sharing

of truth can be hindered not only by misunderstanding, but also by systematic distortion caused by
particular power relationships. Here we are entering the realm of praxis, the realm of relationships
between persons involved in the institutions and
structures of our communities.

Jurgen Habermas, one of the foremost critics of
ideology in Europe and America, has pointed out the
social and political dimension of the dialogical
process. The emphasis is on the situation of
interaction in which the meaning of a text is
understood. Habermas stresses the conditions of
unconstrained and unrestricted discourse in order
that valid truth can be established. All
participants in the community must have the same
opportunity to initiate and be involved in the discussion. They must have the same chance to express
attitudes, ideas and feelings. Barriers which
cause a breakdown in communication must be removed.
Ideology is thus defined as "false consciousness"
or "systematically distorted communication." Self-
reflection and critique must occur in order to
establish the institutional interests and concerns
which influence the communication process.
Habermas insists that no interpretation is value-
free. The aim of the critique is an understanding
of social relationships through analysis and
explanation of the elements of repression,
violence, and coercion within the community, in
order to free it through emancipative action.

For Habermas it is important not only to understand the interpretations of the past, but to
transform the society of the present. Theory and
praxis cannot be separated when we realize that the
community is made up of individuals all participa-
ting in a vast network of power relationships in
both society and church which will influence the
hermeneutic process. Attention must be given to
institutional structures and their use of power so
that implicit ideological biases can be exposed.

Feminist theology insists that of basic importance in realizing how power relationships distort
the communication process is to understand the pervasive influence of patriarchy on both our society
and church. By patriarchy is meant "not only the
subordination of females to males, but the whole
structure of Father-ruled society: aristocracy

over serfs, masters over slaves, kings over subjects, racial overlords over colonized people."[8]
Women have become conscious of how this hierarchical stratification has led to female alienation,[9]
marginalization and exploitation. The vital
inter-subjective dialogue between women and men is
basically affected by power relationships which are
usually only unconsciously sensed and rarely
articulated or taken into account. Feminists thus
begin their interpretations with a "hermeneutic of
suspicion" which helps them uncover areas of self-[10]
interest in the dominant interpretations. They
search carefully to see how biblical texts function
in their original historical-biblical settings as
well as in the ongoing socialization of men and
women. They insist on honesty in spelling out
presuppositions with their ideological and political implication. And they strive for a hermeneutic
community of equality and mutuality where dialogue
can lead to a richer understanding of the text
because all participate equally.

Mennonites who want to interpret the Bible in
community will need to come to terms with patriarchy and its pervasive influence in both church and
society. They will have to examine their structures and institutions realizing how they affect
community dialogue. They will have to become
sensitive to unconscious power relationships which
inhibit free exchange of ideas. They will need to
work for an end to hierarchical structures, sub-
stituting relationships of mutuality and coopera-
tion. Community praxis will then take its proper
place in the hermeneutic process.

3.  Communal language
    The philosopher and theologian Paul Ricoeur has
pointed out the importance of communal language in
the interpretive process.[11] For it is within language that biblical interpretation is made public,
and intersubjectively shared--where religious experience is articulated. It is language that
explains and describes, but also inspires and
manifests. It is language that mediates the meaning of the biblical texts. Ricoeur has looked
carefully at the process of bringing the meaning of
a text back into speech which can be understood.
He recognizes the various types of discourse in our

communities that reactualize the text for our
time--theological reflection and explanation, but
also preaching and poetic discourse.

Ricoeur has focused particularly on symbolic
language with its revelatory and mediatory charac-
teristics.  For symbols represent language in its
most intensive level, language closest to the root
of existence. Their interpretation cannot stay at
the literal level, but must always go beyond to
secondary meanings. These can best be expressed in
ever-expanding metaphorical expressions and concepts.  He notes the richness of biblical language
which includes such complex forms of discourse as
narrative, prophecies, law, proverbs, prayers,
hymns, liturgical writings and wisdom literature.
However when Ricoeur looks at the discourse present
in our scholarly communities, he notes a loss of
sensitivity to poetic and symbolic language.[12]  The
ideal language for persons in the twentieth century
is scientific language which attempts to eradicate
all ambiguity and misunderstanding.  Words and
sentences are explained and defined to ensure
identity of meaning for everyone. Metaphor and
symbol are seen as mere emotional embellishment,
appealing to subjective understanding, not really
having to do with reality.

This linguistic impoverishment in many communities has deprived people of articulating such
existential realities as radical evil or grace-
empowered hope.  Ricoeur recognizes the need for
language that can explain and describe, but also
calls for language that can release the revelatory
power of the text in multiple symbolic and metaphorical expressions.  This is particularly true
for texts which "name God," for though God is named
in diverse ways in the Bible, there is also an
incompleteness about all of these namings. Just as
the kingdom of God is signified through parables,
proverbs and paradoxes for which no literal translations will ever suffice, so no naming of God will
exhaust the meaning of that expression.

The area of language has become increasingly
important in feminist thought. It is not only the
use of inclusive language when referring to persons
that is important.  The most important critiques
are in the whole realm of God-talk. Women have
begun to recognize the poverty of much of the lan-

guage used for God in our communities. As they
point out the narrow and limited male expressions
referring to God which are generally used in our
churches and theological communities, they are also
becoming aware that the traditional doctrinal and
historical-scientific language for God is inadequate.[13]      It is no accident that feminists are
stressing not only expository and creedal formulations of theology but also music, litany, art,
poetry, dance, story, and discussion. The use of
metaphor and parable are highlighted rather than
systematic or syllogistic thought.

Feminist theology is thus making us aware again
of the elusive and mysterious nature of truth. It
is questioning the validity of the prevalent mode
of discourse in both our scholarly and church communities which tries to define and describe God so
literally that many people experience no sense of
relatedness to such a deity. Feminist theologians
have pointed out how interpreters can so identify
God with language about God that one name for God
is absolutized, thus excluding complementary models
and images. They insist that the relationship
between God and human beings is an event, dynamic
and alive; therefore no doctrinal formula or even
symbol or metaphor will be adequate to express its
meaning. As the hermeneutic community of women and
men dialogue about their grace experiences of God
in light of Scripture, new models, metaphors and
concepts will appear. Thus feminists are helping
theology realize the limitedness of its language.
This includes the question of the relationship
between language and the experience it can
mediate--the relationship between theological God-
talk and life's experience of the divine.

Mennonites have traditionally rejected
philosophically-based theology and have prided
themselves on their biblically-based practical
theology. They have rejected symbolic language in
favor of the concrete language of "following
Jesus." At the same time they have been influenced
by various streams of theological thinking,
particularly those that stressed literalistic
interpretation of Scripture or the factually
oriented language of science. God-talk in our communities, both scholarly and congregational, has
tended to become narrow and limited.

As feminists begin to point out the fact that this God-talk is mostly male-oriented, Mennonites will also have to grapple with the mode of discourse best suited for speaking about God. What kind of experience of God does our language express and inspire? How meaningful is our language for contemporary women and men? Is there a richness in our language which can mediate experiences of the transcendent? The focus by feminists on communal language can give Mennonites the opportunity to examine our mode of discourse to see whether we have not succumbed to the sin of idolatry as well as the sin of irrelevance.[14]

In speaking about the importance of the community of faith in the interpretive process, Mennonites have realized that revelational truth emerges in concrete particular communities. They have stressed that God's disclosure in the past and God's work among people in the present come together as the Bible is interpreted in the community of believers. They have recognized that salvific experiences can open a community to understanding the truth in the Scripture. Women are now beginning to share experiences of liberation and salvation with their faith communities. As they do so, communal traditions, communal structures and institutions, and communal language will be challenged by their insights and critiques. The opportunity is there for us to experience anew the dynamic on-going presence of God who continues to work creatively in our communities of faith.

## Notes

1. This perspective is articulated in a number of the essays in Willard Swartley, ed. Essays on Biblical Interpretation: Anabaptist-Mennonite Perspectives (Elkhart, Indiana:   Institute of Mennonite Studies, 1984).   Note particularly the essays by Walter Klaassen and John Howard Yoder.

2. Sheila D. Collins, "Feminist Theology at the Crossroads," Christianity and Crisis, Dec. 14, 1981, p. 344.   Note also the way Elizabeth Schüssler Fiorenza points out the importance of the communal base for Scripture interpretation in Bread Not Stone (Boston:  Beacon Press, 1984), 41-42.

3. Letty M. Russell, "Authority and the Challenge of Feminist Interpretation" in Feminist Interpretation of the Bible, ed. Letty M. Russell (Philadelphia:  Westminster Press, 1985), 142.

4. Hans-Georg Gadamer, Truth and Method (London:   Sheed and Ward, 1975).  Note particularly pp. 271-274.

5. Rosemary Radford Ruether, "Feminist Interpretation:   A Method of Correlation" in Feminist Interpretation of the Bible, 112.

6. Elizabeth Schüssler Fiorenza has begun this work in her book In Memory of Her (New York: Crossroad, 1984).

7. See Jurgen Habermas, Theory and Practice (Boston:   Beacon Press, 1973), 1-40, and Knowledge and Human Interest (Boston:  Beacon Press, 1968).

8. Rosemary Radford Ruether, Sexism and God-talk (Boston:  Beacon Press, 1983), 61.

9. This is particularly true in theological education.   However women are beginning to articulate their struggle to gain a valid place in the theological process.  See the Cornwall Collective, Your Daughters Shall Prophesy:   Feminist Alternatives in Theological Education (New York:   Pilgrim Press, 1980).

10. Elizabeth Schüssler Fiorenza, In Memory of Her, p. xxiii.

11. Paul Ricoeur elaborates on these theories in a number of books and articles.  Among the most helpful are:  Interpretation Theory:  Discourse and the Surplus of Meaning (Fort Worth, Texas:  Texas Christian University Press, 1976); "Naming God,"

Union Seminary Quarterly Review XXXIV, No. 4 (Summer 1979).

12. Lewis S. Mudge, "Paul Ricoeur on Biblical Interpretation" in Essays on Biblical Interpretation, Paul Ricoeur (Philadelphia: Fortress Press, 1980), 4, 5.

13. Sallie McFague, Metaphorical Language: Models of God in Religious Language (Philadelphia: Fortress Press, 1982), 4-7. An example of feminists working at the question of God language particularly in worship is Image-Breaking/Image-Building, by Linda Clark, Marian Ronan and Eleanor Walker (New York: Pilgrim Press), 1981.

14. Sallie McFague, Metaphorical Language, 4-9.

## THE NEW TESTAMENT HAUSTAFEL:
## EGALITARIAN OR STATUS QUO?

By David Schroeder

Luther called the sections in Ephesians/ Colossians/1 Peter, which speak to the relations of wife-husband, slave-master, parent-child, and the citizen to government, a Haustafel. In English literature they have been called "Household Precepts," "Household Codes," "Domestic Codes" or "Station Codes."

Few New Testament passages have been used so frequently to champion non-Christian and unethical causes than these Haustafeln. They have been used to support 1) the patriarchal family pattern, 2) the subjugation of women in society, 3) the integration of Christians with society (status quo), 4) blind obedience to the state, and 5) the enslavement of people including the slave trade.

We should have been forewarned early that to give a status quo reading of the Haustafel was not tenable. When Wilberforce and others challenged the institution of slavery, they called for a different reading of the Haustafel. When the confessing church in Germany realized that they could in no way give blind obedience to the Hitler regime, it recognized that the Haustafel needed a different interpretation. For the sake of consistency, this material should also be reexamined with regard to the place of women in society. In fact, the basic understanding of the NT Haustafel needs to be reworked. This reworking has already begun, but not always in the right direction.

My concern has been to work out a proper frame-of-reference within which to interpret the Haustafel. To do this, I have chosen to look particularly at the Haustafel material in 1 Peter.

### The Question of Pre-understanding (Vorverständnis)

Most of the outcomes of the process of interpretation are determined by our pre-understanding-- the things that are assumed but not argued in the exegesis. To a large extent the frame-of-reference which we bring to a passage determines our find-

ings.    It   is  legitimate, therefore, to ask questions  about   the   pre-understandings  we  bring to
specific   texts.    For example, throughout the history  of   the  Church (apart from the early Church)
the   patriarchal   structure of the family was never
really  questioned.    It  never occurred to people
that "Wives be subject to your husbands" could mean
anything but obedience and subservience to husbands
or  that "Be subject to every human institution, to
the   Emperor   as   Supreme"  could mean anything but
total   allegiance   to  government.  The question of
civil disobedience did not arise!

My  disagreement  with  this traditional interpretation  centers  mainly on the assumptions which
are  brought  to  the  text.   In this paper I will
assume that the context in which the Haustafel came
into being was not from stoic philosophy as held by
K. Weidinger and M. Dibelius and still followed in
E. Lohse,  nor  from Philo, as held by J. Crouch,$^2$
but  from  the  exhortations given to Greek Gentile
Christians  as answers to their questions about how
to  live  in society, questions about their station
in life as followers of Christ, and their desire to
live  as  Christians  in society.  My assumption is
that the time of writing 1 Peter (i.e. in what context of persecution 1 Peter was written) was not in
the  latter part of the first century as a response
to  the  persecution under Domitian, or even in the
second  century,  but  in  the time from 69-75 A.D.
when the persecutions originated not from the state
but from the general populous.

Scholars also differ in their assumptions about
what  the 1 Peter Haustafel was said to accomplish.
D. Balch and Elizabeth Schüssler Fiorenza interpret
the  1 Peter Haustafel as defending the status quo,
as  advocating  the  abandonment of all egalitarian
notions  propagated  in  the early missionary movement,  and  as  advising Christians to accept again
the  patriarchal  structure of  society  so  as to
reduce or alleviate the severity of the persecution
they  were  suffering.[3]   This position is not con-
vincing.

J.  H.  Elliott's assumption, that the 1 Peter
Haustafel  was calling on Christians to bring a new
ethic to the structures of society and thus be witnesses  to  their faith in Christ even in difficult
situations  of  persecution,  seems much more credible.[4]

Leonhard Goppelt sees the purpose of the 1
Peter Haustafel in terms of the Two Kingdom Theory
of Luther.   Seen thus, the Haustafel provides a
personal ethic for Christians that may be quite
different from the ethic exercised by the same person in his/her involvements in society and when
engaged in public service. He reads it very much
as a "station code," a code that indicates how
Christians are to live in society. But by being
fully integrated with society, the main ethic of
the Haustafel is lost.

## The Case for an Egalitarian Reading.
    1.  The Purpose for Writing
    As J. H. Elliott has shown, the letter of 1
Peter clearly assumed that despite persecution,
Christians are to be witnesses to Christ in the
world.   The main purpose of the writer of the
epistle is stated in 2:4-10, the passage that
immediately precedes the Haustafel. This paragraph
ended with the admonition "that you may declare the
deeds of him who called you out of darkness into
his marvelous light."   In like manner, in the
introduction to the Haustafel (2:11-12) the idea of
witness was central: "Maintain good conduct among
the Gentiles, so that in case they speak against
you as evildoers, they may see your good deeds and
glorify God on the day of visitation."
    Furthermore, after the conclusion of the
Haustafel the writer again returned to the theme of
witnessing: "Always be prepared to make a defense
to anyone who calls you to account for the hope
that is in you, yet do it with gentleness and
reverence" (3:15). The context clearly suggested
that Christians are to be witnesses for Christ in
their stations in life as they continue their
involvement in society.
    Thus, it is unlikely that the writer was call-
ing for a lesser ethic than that which had already
been proclaimed in the missionary communities.
Rather, the author knew how difficult it would be
for people who had no power to remain true to their
faith in the stations which they were powerless to
change.   He thus exhorted them to continue to be
faithful to Christ in spite of harassment and persecution.

2. The Historical Context

At the time of the writing of 1 Peter certain expectations of behavior were placed on all members of society.

a) Proper worship of the Emperor could not be avoided. From early on Augustus had required a daily sacrifice for the Emperor in the temple at Jerusalem. No doubt Paul was aware of Caligula's attempt to place a bust of himself in the Temple. The Emperor cult was especially strong in Asia Minor. What others assumed to be a self-evident practice, worship of the Emperor, was now being asked of the Jewish and Christian communities. Because the Christians could not fulfill these expectations, hostilities arose.

b) Religious syncretism was the norm. <u>Not</u> to worship all the gods was taken as a sign of irreligion. In this situation the Jewish and Christian faith as well as the Isis and Dionysiac cults did not conform. They were consequently seen as irreligious, and as a threat to the total society.

c) The household or "house" was a basic unit of society. The "house" consisted not only of the extended family but included all the slaves and servants as well. A large house could have several hundred to a thousand people in it. The master, or head of the house, ruled over the whole house. He (and in isolated cases she) not only determined what work should be done, and delegated such responsibilities to various persons, but also determined issues of faith and practice. If the master converted to Judaism or Christianity, he could bring the whole house into that faith with him. It was expected of all people to honor and abide by the structure of the house. But problems arose when an individual converted to Christianity and stayed in the house especially if the head of the house was not a Christian. In this instance conflict could not very well be avoided.

d) The house was considered to be the microcosm of the macrocosm. What the house was on a small scale was what the society would be on a larger scale. Thus if the order of the house would be changed, all of society would change. Therefore, if you brought disorder to the house, you would bring anarchy to the nation state or city state.

D. Balch has shown that the topics, "Concerning the State," "Concerning Household Management" and "Concerning Marriage" were still strongly represented in the Aristotelian-Platonic tradition and that the conversion of subordinate members of the house to another faith was seen as a revolutionary, subversive act.[7] E. Fiorenza basically agrees with this finding.[8]

It can be assumed that in relation to the synagogue and in relation to the Christian missionary work, when heads of households converted to Judaism and Christianity, subordinate persons in those households normally converted as well. If the head of the house converted to Christianity, few problems resulted, because the house simply became a house-church. It was very different, however, when subordinates in a household in which the house remained non-Christian converted to Christianity. For slaves in such a house to convert to Christianity did not hold out many good prospects. They would certainly be persecuted. Yet we see no encouragement in 1 Peter for such persons to give up the faith nor to become disobedient to Christ. What we see rather is strong encouragement for the converts to keep the faith and to suffer the consequences for their obedience to Christ.

3. Responsible Christian Action

What was responsible Christian action in this context? Those who came out of a Greek background and had accepted Christ wanted to know their new moral responsibilities in Christ. This applied especially to those stations which did not enjoy full moral responsibility: slaves, women, aliens. These converts to Christ were immediately aware that they could no longer determine their moral responsibility by simply asking what was reasonable or natural for them to do in their station, as they had done previously. As soon as they converted to Christianity, new Christians began to relate ethics to Christ. The epistle of 1 Peter addresses new Christians and their ethical responsibility. a) The primary ethic was that of obedience to Christ (1:1, 14, 22). They were to put off their former practices and live according to the will of God (2:1-3, 4:2). The will of God with respect to basic social responsibility, was spelled out for

them in the Haustafel. All of it assumed that
ultimate obedience belonged to Christ.

b) They were called to be Christian in every
station in life. The author addressed the readers
in terms of their stations in life, stations they
were powerless to change. Of each one he required
personal, moral responsibility. In a sense he was
giving power (i.e. moral responsibility) to the
powerless through his exhortations.

This charge to "aliens," "slaves" and "wives"
to make personal moral judgments and to make personal decisions as to what to do came as a surprise
to them and to society. To exercise such moral
responsibility, they had to break with the structures of that society. Just to retain their faith
in Christ was already to break with the structures,
a break that was not kindly received.

c) They were exhorted to "be subject." The
exhortation to "be subject" in all of the subordinate stations comes as a bit of a surprise to us
today. We are surprised because throughout the
Christian era this has been understood in terms of
obedience, or blind allegiance rather than submission. But this is to misunderstand what was said.

To be subject to the state did not mean blind
and unquestioning obedience. It meant the acknowl-
edgement of a structure that one was powerless to
change but under which one must nevertheless take
responsibility for one's actions. And we are never
without such structures or human institutions
(2:13).

Not to admonish people to be subject to the
powers would have meant to advocate revolt or
revolution in the pattern of the Zealots. Not to
counsel the slave to be subject to the master would
be like saying to a Christian laborer today not to
be a laborer, i.e. that no Christian should be a
laborer. Where would you go as a wife if you dis-
regarded the structure of the family and the house?
An alternate option would first of all have to be
created. Such an alternate setting was in fact
created in the Christian "house-church." The
writer was, however, not writing to those who were
in Christian houses-churches but to those in non-
Christian houses. The admonition to "be subject"
recognized the fact that there were structures of
order in the society and that those structures were

often oppressive and unjust. Therefore the
exhortation to "be subject" (to the master, and to
the husband) and to bring a new ethic to each station were not incompatible.

The exhortation to "be subject" was a call to
operate on three levels at once in such difficult
situations. i) The level of the ideal of equality
was stated in Galatians 3:28. There it was indi-
cated that there is neither Jew nor Greek, bond nor
free, male or female in Christ. All were equal.
All were moral persons with full responsibility for
their actions. ii) In the arena of the Christian
fellowship a new life and new egalitarian structures could be modeled. Here women and slaves in
fact had a new status in the church. They were
joint heirs of the grace of life (3:7). iii) In
the arena of the world, in the larger society, they
did not have the power to change things except
indirectly. In society, Christians including
slaves and women, acted in terms of doing what was
right and taking the consequences for their
actions. They depended on people seeing the new
life modeled in their own lives and in the Church,
and trusting that this new model would be seen as a
new and better form of life and thus become accep-
table to the larger community. Here they could
only let their light shine (3:22).

4. The Requirement to Do Good.

Every time "be subject" is mentioned it was
equally underlined that believers were "to do what
was right." The writer also reminded them that
they would have to suffer for it. It was assumed
that they were free to choose the good and to act
on it (2:15). The author knew that the Christian
slaves would have to suffer for doing good and
reassured them with the words "to this you have
been called" (2:21). Hardly any of the writers on
1 Peter notice the combination of "be subject" and
"do good/right," yet the whole letter focuses on
this combination. The whole point of the letter
was to encourage Christians in a very difficult and
powerless situation to remain responsible Christians and to suffer for doing the right and not for
doing what is wrong. Thus every person addressed
was addressed as a fully moral person.

5. Follow the Example of Christ.

Nothing was more powerful in supporting the

writer's message than the reference to Christ in connection with his exhortation to the slave (2:21-25). Nothing was more forboding in its consequences than for a slave to break with the structures of society. It could well mean the loss of life. It was precisely in this setting that the writer reminded the slaves of Jesus. Jesus too was subject to the powers-that-be; he too broke with the structures of society; he too suffered and was put to death. But the point was that he overcame evil with good, and that he trusted God who judges impartially and justly (2:23). He modeled a new way for the Christians.

This calls on us to use the earthly life and experience of Jesus much more in exegeting what it really means to be faithful disciples in a society that rejects the Christian way.

6. The Way of Suffering and Service.

Although the call to follow the example of Christ was given in the exhortation to the Christian slaves, it was paradigmatic of the whole sequence. The writer suggested that God's will for the Christian life, including the exhortation to "be subject" and to "do what was right," was supremely manifested in the life of Jesus. The way that the "powerless" in society were to take was the way the "powerless" Jesus walked--the way of service and suffering:

> Who did no sin, neither was guile found in his mouth: Who, when he was reviled, reviled not again; when he suffered, he threatened not; but committed himself to him that judgeth righteously: Who his own self bare our sins in his own body on the tree, that we, being dead to sins, should live unto righteousness: by whose stripes ye were healed (1 Pet. 2:22-25).

This was the model of being subject to the powers, the model of self-less service to others, the model of resistance and non-resistance, the model of challenging others through doing good. It was also the model for bearing the sins of others through suffering and forgiveness.

To follow this model was to give full moral responsibility to those who were not held to be free and accountable; it was a way of giving power to the powerless. What it called for was to do

what was right, to take the consequences for such
actions and to trust in God who judges justly
(2:23).

    7. The Requirement to Act on the Basis of the
Victory of Christ.

    There was an eschatological side to this ethic
that should not be neglected. Christians had a new
and living hope through the resurrection (1:3).
Since Christ suffered and died for the sins of all,
the righteous for the unrighteous, he was also
raised to newness of life and so overcame sin and
death (3:18). This victory was an encouragement to
those who were now suffering for their obedience to
Christ, since they could fully expect to share in
his victory. Christians were able to do what was
right and to walk in the resurrection because they
were assured of the victory of Christ and the
establishment of his reign.

## Conclusion

    The Haustafel must be seen in terms of the new
ethic of the early Christian missionaries. It is
in full continuum with that ethic. In fact, it
speaks directly to those in subordinate stations
who felt the full brunt of persecution because of
their obedience to Christ and because of their
break with the structures of society.

    This conclusion is supported by the fact that
slaves and women were addressed as morally
responsible persons, as being able to choose to act
contrary to the expectations of society, as being
able to retain their own faith in a non-Christian
"house," as those who did what was right even if
that was seen as a sign of irreligion if not
treason. The Haustafel in no way supported the
status quo. It encouraged and empowered persons in
subordinate stations to fully own and act on their
own moral responsibility to God and to other persons.

## Notes

1. David   Schroeder, Die Haustafeln des Neuen
Testaments  Ihres  herkunft  und Ihr theologischer
Sinn  (Hamburg,  1959, unpublished diss.).  J. Paul
Sampley, 'And the Two Shall Become One Flesh' (NY:
Cambridge  University  Press, 1971).  James Crouch,
The Origin and Intention of the Colossian Haustafel
(Göttingen:     Vandenhoeck  and  Ruprecht,  1972).
David Balch, Let Wives be Submissive:  The Domestic
Code  in  1  Peter.     (Chico,  CA:  Scholars Press
1981).
2.  Karl  Weidinger, Die Haustafeln.  En Stück
unchristlicher Paränese (Leipzig 1928).  Martin Di-
belius, An die kolosser Epheser an Philemon  (Hand-
buch zum Neuen Testament) 3rd Ed. (Tübingen:  J. C.
B. LeMohr, 1953).  Crouch, op.cit and Eduard Lohse,
Die Briefe an die Kolosser und an Philemon
(Göttingen:  Vandenhoeck and Ruprecht, 1968).
3.  Elizabeth  Schüssler Fiorenza, In Memory of
Her:  A  Feminist  Theological  Reconstruction of
Christian  Origins  (London:     SCM  1983).  Balch,
op.cit.
4. A  Home  for  the  Homeless:  A Sociological
Exegesis of 1 Peter, Its  Situation  and Strategy
(Philadelphia:  Fortress, 1981).
5.  Der    Erste  Petrus  Brief,  ed.  F. Hahn.
(Göttingen:  Vandenhoeck and Ruprecht, 1978).
6.  Elliott,  op.cit.  21ff on Ockos, paraockos.
Hans-Josef  Klauck,  Hausgemeinde und Hauskirche im
frühen   Christenturm  (Stuttgart:     Katholisches
Bibelwerk, 1981).
7.  Balch,  "Let Wives Be Submissive. . ." The
Origin, Form and Apologetic Function of the Household  Duty  Code (Haustafel) in 1 Peter (Ann Arbor:
University Microfilms International, 1976) 176ff.
8.  Fiorenza, op.cit., 255-264.

# THE TRIUMPHAL ENTRY: A STUDY OF AUTHORITY
## Luke 19:28-21:38

Mary Schertz

Letty Russell has a section in her book Feminist Interpretation of the Bible entitled "Feminists at Work." I like her image of the workshop and I conceptualize my task as inviting you into my workshop to look at three projects-in-progress and to help me evaluate that progress.

The projects are all different, and as I have thought about them I have realized that the typology for feminist uses of biblical materials developed by Katharine Sakenfeld in Russell's book fits well what I do. Professor Sakenfeld lists three ways feminists commonly use Scripture: 1) looking to texts about women to counteract famous texts used "against" women, 2) looking to the Bible generally for a theological perspective offering a critique of patriarchy, and 3) looking to texts about women to learn from history and stories. Sakenfeld lists the strengths and weaknesses of each of the approaches in a clear and forthright manner.

In this paper I will be exploring the second approach which Sakenfeld calls: "looking to the Bible generally for a theological perspective offering a critique of patriarchy." I will be using the triumphal entry story in Luke and looking primarily at the way the issues of power and authority are interwoven in the text.

The section of Luke in which our passage appears (Luke 19:28-21:38) may be called the Olivet section because, as you will notice, Luke 19:28 decribes Jesus approaching "Bethphage and Bethany at the hill called Olivet..." and Luke 21:38 describes him teaching in the temple by day and going on to the hill called Olivet at night. This inclusio involving the place name Olivet marks the section as a literary unit and indicates that it deserves to be regarded as a whole.

The section begins with the triumphal entry into Jerusalem, Jesus' weeping over the city and his cleansing of the temple (19:29-48). Subsequently, various groups challenge, in a variety of ways, the authority exhibited by Jesus in the events of his entry into the city. These challenges, along with Jesus' responses to them, comprise the middle portion of the text (20:1-21:4). The text concludes with an

apocalyptic sermon (21:5-36) which Jesus delivers to
those who call him "Teacher" (21:7). As noted earlier, these three sections--the first narrative, the
second dialogical, and the third didactic--are en-
compassed within a framework (19:28, 29 and 21:37, 38)
which places the events in the proximity of Olivet, a
place to which Jesus returns each night after teaching
in the temple during the day.

Since the issues of power and authority are central to both feminist concerns and to this text, we
will begin our inquiry with a set of sociological
questions: In this text, who has power? What kind of
power is it? When is it used? Why? What are the
consequences? Who is effectual? Who is not?

We can divide these questions into two processes:
first we will ask the descriptive question: What
sorts of consequences and changes does the text
portray as brought about by the exercise of authority?
Second, we will ask the analytical question: What
sorts of power are presupposed by the text as the
"source which backs and sustains these consequences
and changes?"

My thesis is that this text establishes a hierarchy of competing powers in which the exercise of
authority to effect change at one level is thwarted or
sanctioned by the exercise of authority at the next
level. These exercises of authority, in order of
their ascending degrees of ability are performed by:
1) "officers" such as Pharisees, Sadducees, chief
priests, scribes and elders; 2) the people; 3) agents
of Jesus such as the disciples; 4) Jesus; 5) cosmic
powers.

Let's look, briefly, at each of these categories.
For the sake of time, I will be focusing primarily on
the narrative section (19:28-48) although we certainly
need to keep the larger literary unit in mind as we
make our observations and draw our conclusions. The
first category, the officers, make their appearance in
the context of the entry into Jerusalem. At the
climax of that scene, when the "multitude of the disciples" proclaims Jesus' kingship, the Pharisees tell
Jesus to rebuke them. Jesus replies that if the disciples were quiet the stones would "cry out" (19:37-
40). The text records no consequence of the
Pharisees' attempt to exercise their authority. This
ineffectiveness of the Pharisees' authority re-echoes
in the ineffectiveness of the "chief priests and

scribes and principal men of the people" who, in vv.
47, 48 respond to Jesus' cleansing of the temple by
seeking to destroy him. According to Luke, "they did
not find anything they could do, for all the people
hung upon his words." Thus the text opposes the purposes and intents of these official types with the
purposes and intents of the multitude of disciples and
people, who comprise the second category of authority.
Not only does the text oppose these two classes of
people, but the officers' attempts to exercise their
authority to silence the people and to kill Jesus are
thwarted by the people. The people's power to effect
consequences is greater than that of the officers, and
since the purposes of the two types conflict, the consequences by which the story progresses are those
effected by the power of the people. Because the
people "hang on his words" the officers cannot do anything to destroy Jesus. Because he is not destroyed,
Jesus continues to teach the people in the temple.

The third level of the hierarchy of authority
involves the agents of Jesus. In the case of the narrative section at which we are looking most closely,
the agents are the disciples. Later, the parable of
the vineyard and tenants plays the same role of Jesus'
agent. The story Jesus tells has power over the
people who then, in turn, exercise power over the
officers. In this case, however, it is the disciples.
When the disciples untie the colt (19:33), they come
up against the resistance of the owners in the same
way that the crowd's proclamation of Jesus' kingship
came up against the resistance of the Pharisees. But
when the disciples respond to this resistance by
saying "the Lord has need of it" (as they were
instructed to do), they are able to bring the colt
(19:29-35). Because they are Jesus' agents, they are
able to overcome the resistance and complete the deed.
Thus the exercise of this authority involves the
invocation of Jesus' name—rather than proclamation or
adoration as did the authority exercised by the crowds
at the second level.

The fourth category of authority presented by the
text is the authority exercised by Jesus himself.
Jesus effects consequences and changes by: 1) direct-
ing agents, as in his instructing the two disciples to
get the colt; 2) attracting/permitting acclamation,
as in the entry into Jerusalem, and adoration, as evi-
denced by the people who "hung upon his words;" 3)

dis-empowering the Pharisees through verbal repartee,
as in his reply about the stones crying out. We might
note parenthetically that Jesus' ability to outwit his
opponents and his use of that ability becomes a major
emphasis in the next section of the text.

In addition to effecting consequences in these
ways, Jesus effects change through indirect action.
For example, Jesus initiates consequences simply by
"going up" to Jerusalem (19:28), and by choosing
proximity to the temple, where, for example, certain
actions bear a kind of significance they would not
bear in other locations. Jesus also initiates consequences by entering the city in a certain manner--
riding a colt spread with garments and accompanied by
disciples acclaiming his kingship (19:29-40). The
initiation of this action has a very direct and
immediate consequence in the rebuke delivered by the
Pharisees (40). Finally, Jesus initiates consequences
by entering the temple and driving out the merchants
(45, 46). According to the text, there are two
immediate consequences of this action: 1) Jesus
establishes residence in the temple and 2) a con-
spiracy forms against him (47). By juxtaposing
actions (direct and indirect) with consequences in
this manner, the text makes it very clear that,
whether the consequences are positive or negative,
they are regulated by the intents and purposes of
Jesus himself. Jesus is therefore portrayed as exer-
cising an authority in keeping with his particular
position in the hierarchy established by the text. He
performs actions that effect consequences which must
be taken into account by himself and all those "below"
him in the hierarchy of authority.

Having defined Jesus as the fourth level of
authority in the text, the question remains whether
there is any sort of authority positioned above Jesus
in the hierarchy. I would argue that there is,
indeed, such an authority. In 19:41-44, Luke portrays
Jesus pausing as he draws near to Jerusalem and weeping. Jesus then delivers a kind of monologue which
begins with the conditional phrase, "if you knew the
things that make for peace" (42) and ends with the
condemnation "you did not know the time of your
visitation," which I think refers to Jesus himself as
the unrecognized visitor to Jerusalem. Thus there is
an inclusio on the basis of the verb egnos (you knew).
Bracketed within these two "not-knowings" are several

predictions addressed to the city of Jerusalem.
Because Jerusalem does not know, or recognize the
situation correctly, it will be surrounded by its
enemies and dashed to the ground, left without "one
stone upon another" (44).

On the basis of these observations, I am suggesting that the evils of war and destruction seem to be
marked as (or contained within) the result of not
recognizing Jesus and his importance. Jesus does not
himself assume control over these cosmic powers--
indeed for him to do so would deny Jerusalem's
prerogative to accept or reject him. But he plays a
role in that grander design--as the vision of the "Son
of Man" returning in glory at the end of the passage
clearly indicates.

At this point, we have looked at the kinds of consequences and changes effected by the various kinds of
authority exercised within the narratival section of
the text under consideration. These authorities in a
descending order of efficacy might be listed as: cosmic powers of good and evil with God in control;
Jesus; Jesus' agents; the people; and the "officers."

With that description in mind, we are now ready to
ask the more analytical question of what sorts of
power are presupposed by the text as the "source which
backs and sustains these consequences and changes."

I propose that for heuristic purposes we look at a
sociological description of power. John H. Schütz, a
Pauline scholar has suggested some helpful categories.
He defines implicit sources of authority as those
considered to be basic to the fact of social organization itself: "Authority rests within the social
organization and is constantly being underwritten by
those who command and those who obey, presumably
because the goals of the social organization benefit
and are shared by both."

While the fact that most of the authority we experience in daily life has this implicit nature is
obvious, it does not explain how a "rationale of
authority" may exist outside such social frameworks
and may even contribute to the building up of social
organization itself. Implicitness does not explain
how power becomes implicit in the social structure.

According to Schütz, the terms "proximate" and
"ultimate" describe two ways in which authority that
is not implicit in social structures can be expressed
or established. A proximate source of authority is

one based on reason, one in which the persons seeking
to gain obedience are authorities to the extent that
they can elaborate the reasons for their will, though
they need not always do so. This sort of authority
"requires that those who receive the communication
recognize in it a relationship to knowledge they possess and values or beliefs they share".[3]  In other
words, it makes sense and the person holding the power
holds it only insofar as it continues to make sense.

Whereas proximate authority is based on a communication of reason, ultimate authority is based on a
communication of power itself.   In this case, the
authority is based on the perception that power is
"available and effective for the purposes the authority has in mind" whatever those purposes may be.
Another word to describe this kind of power might be
"charismatic" in a social, not religious, sense.

When we apply these three notions about the
sources of authority to our text, the first thing we
notice is that the kind of authority the text has
identified as least effective, simply because the purposes and intentions of the actors are consistently
thwarted by the exercise of an authority or authorities higher on the text's hierarchy, is an implicit
authority.  At least I suggest that the Pharisees--as
the text portrays them in verse 39, for example--as
well as the "chief priests and scribes and the principal men of the people" represent implicit sources of
authority.   Their attempts to command are based upon
the assumption that the fulfillment of their will is
in keeping with the goals of the social organization.
While development of what those goals are is beyond
the scope of this project, we may assume that because
these actors are identified by their social status or
function that they do indeed represent implicit
sources of authority.

The authority identified as "the people" is also
an implicit authority, but the text captures it in a
different stage of the social process. As Schütz
notes, implicit authority is "underwritten by those
who command and those who obey."[4]   Whereas the
officers are attempting, in their exercise of authority, to maintain this mutual project, the people are
at least beginning to withdraw their consent from the
arrangement.   This withdrawal is explicit in the disciples' acclamation of Jesus' kingship. This acclamation establishes a new source of authority that, as

Schütz points out, has the potential "to call into existence alternative social structures." The fact that the acclamation involves kingship, a term with heavy social and political connotations, underscores this point. The effects of the people's authority is evident in v. 48 where the officers are disempowered— "they did not find anything they could do, for all the people hung upon his words." We might say, therefore, that the lowest two levels of the text's hierarchy of authority represent both aspects of the mutual project (command and obedience) which ground implicit authority. In addition, the text portrays this kind of authority in a moment of disintegration.

The next three levels of the hierarchy can, in some senses at least, be treated as an entity. These three levels represent different positions within a framework of ultimate authority. This conclusion is based on two kinds of textual evidence. First, the text defines this authority as being outside the social system. For example, Jesus' instructions about the colt contain no provisions for the proprieties of personal property, a social organization. In fact, his instructions rather pointedly transcend this convention. To the owners' remonstrance, the disciples are to reply: "the Lord has need of it." In addition, the kingship imagery, as noted earlier, defines Jesus' authority as being outside the existing social organization, as does Jesus' prediction of Jerusalem's destruction and his usurpation of the temple.

Second, the text does not define this authority in terms of reason, but rather in terms of power itself. Even in this short text it is clear that the authority is ultimate rather than proximate because Jesus connects his own mission as the unrecognized "visitor" to Jerusalem with the pending cataclysmic judgment. Therefore, even though he gives reasons for driving the merchants out of the temple, for refusing to rebuke the disciples who proclaim him king, and for commandeering the colt, these "reasons" are not real reasons (in the sense of a rationale) but statements about his power.

Having made this case, however, we need to note the logic of power as well. Remember that Schütz describes proximate, or rational power as the sort which establishes, for those who obey, some relationship to their prior knowledge, values and beliefs which makes sense to them. Without getting into the debate among

NT scholars about class stratification in the early
church, we might note that for those who are powerless, any different power can build some rational connection with their own convictions about the source of
their powerlessness. While the nature of authority in
this passage is clearly ultimate, the dynamics of
power/powerlessness may indicate undertones of the
proximate kind of power.

Overall, then, the analysis seems to indicate that
the power implicit in social structures is relativized
by the text while the ultimate power exhibited in the
person and actions of Jesus is idealized.

Now, the question is: what does this story have
to do with us as feminist hermeneuts? Is the gospel
saying that the power implicit in social structures is
evil?    Does the passage give feminists and any other
group which may be dissatisfied with the status quo,
license to subvert these social structures just
because that is what Jesus does when he enters
Jerusalem? Does the passage support anarchy?

The other question to ask is: does the story have
anything at all to do with feminists? After all, in
the passage we've dealt with most closely, no women
appear.    On top of that, one of the major images of
the passage is that of king--a male-dominant image if
there ever was one. What does a passage that contains
no feminist consciousness that I can determine have to
say to us?

I would answer both of those questions in the
negative. The passage does not support anarchy. And
the passage is not irrelevant to feminist concerns.

The key to answering both questions is to note
precisely where Jesus' ultimate authority subverts the
implicit authority of the social structures. The
implicit power of the structures is subverted precisely at the point where that power impeded Jesus'
project:
- his need of a colt
- his progress into the city
- his use of the temple.

At the point where the in-breaking of the Kingdom
is slowed or diminished or hindered in any way, the
ultimate power of God's Spirit must and does take
precedence over the implicit power embedded in our
structures.

Is not the renewed and expanded discipleship of
women, a discipleship abundantly attested in this

gathering of women caring for the church, women working for justice, women thinking theologically, women
studying Scripture, such an in-breaking of the Kingdom
of God?

## Notes

1. "Feminist Uses of Biblical Materials," in Feminist Interpretation of the Bible, ed. Letty M. Russell, (Philadelphia:  Westminster, 1985) 55-64.
2. Paul and the Anatomy of Apostolic Authority
(Cambridge University Press, 1975) 11f.
3. Ibid., 13.
4. Ibid., 11,12.

# LIKEWISE YOU WIVES..."
## ANOTHER LOOK AT 1 Peter 2:11-5:11

### Mary Schertz

I would like to invite you to explore with me a second option for the feminist use of Scripture. According to Katharine Sakenfeld this approach involves "looking to texts about women to counteract famous texts used 'against' women."

1 Peter 2:11-5:11 has been chosen for consideration because 3:1-7 contains one of those injunctions to wives that have proven so problematic for a modern feminist consciousness. This passage also contains injunctions to slaves and to youth in the three-fold pairing: master-slave, husband-wife, parent-child common in Greco-Roman literature, as well as other New Testament texts, and known as the Haustafeln or the Household Codes.

I want to do three things with this passage. First, we will look briefly at the literary arrangement of the piece because I think it is a helpful key to its interpretation. Second, I want to argue that the theme of non-resistance is intricately interwound with the injunctions to slaves and wives, but not with the injunction to the youth. And finally, I want to sketch the implications these findings have for the business with which we are engaged today: the business of feminist hermeneutics.

### Literary Structure.

The first thing we want to note here is the most obvious: in 2:18 there is the injunction to slaves: "servants, be submissive to your masters with all respect...." In 3:1 it says "likewise you wives, be submissive to your husbands." But it is not until 5:5 that the author introduces the last of the traditional three pairings, "Likewise you that are younger be subject to the elders." The question is: why all those words, all those ideas, interjected between the message to the wives and the message to the youth? If you check the Haustafel in Ephesians or Colossians, you will see the difference.

Biblical scholars through the ages, as you might suspect, have tried to explain this matter in all sorts of ways: sometimes along the lines that

75

the author didn't quite know what he was doing or that someone down the line rearranged the text.

I don't think either of those things happened. I want to suggest, at least, that the author was quite intentional about the way he arranged his material and that the arrangement is consistent with the message he wants to communicate.

If we look at the text, we will note that there are two parallel sections: verses 2:11-4:11 compose one of these sections and 4:12-5:11 the other. A number of scholars have proposed these boundaries on thematic grounds. Let me point out briefly a few of the literary reasons why I concur with their judgment:

1. Both passages begin with an endearment. Beloved (agapetoi) in 2:11 and 4:12.

2. Both passages end with a doxology in nearly identical language: "to him belong glory and dominion for ever and ever. Amen." in 4:11. "To him be the dominion for ever and ever. Amen." in 5:11.

3. There is a great deal of repeated vocabulary, especially of such key words as: suffering, doing evil, doing good, "speaking against," and the will of God.

4. There is at least one fairly distinctive word play. In 2:13, toward the beginning of the first section under consideration, the author urges his readers to submit to every human creation (in Greek the word for creation is ktisis). In 4:19, toward the beginning of the second section, the readers are urged to entrust/commit themselves to the faithful Creator (ktiste). While I don't want to push the point too hard, I do think the similarity in the word choice reflects a point the author wants to make. This point might be paraphrased something like this: The human creations, to which the Christians are to be subject are, in turn, themselves subject to the Creator to whom the Christians entrust themselves.

While there might be other parallels between the two passages which we might note, I think these suffice to give us some sense of the way in which the author is orchestrating the broad movements of the body of the piece.

Seeing the artistry with which this work is developed warns us against taking this writer too lightly. This careful work leads us to at least ask the question about whether the fact that the injunctions to slaves and wives belong to one literary unit while the injunction to youth belongs to another means something. In order to answer that question we will need to look more closely at the section containing the problematic injunctions.

First of all, the concept of a ring composition or chiasm is important to an understanding of this passage. A ring composition or a chiasm is a literary construction in which the first line or element of the composition is similar to the last line or element, the second element similar to the second from the end, the third similar to the third from the end, etc. The innermost element may or may not have a counterpart. This construction, common in both testaments, is a device used for emphasis. While there is no hard and fast rule as to whether the chiasm is drawing attention to the innermost element(s) or the outermost, the frame, the individual chiasm usually indicates the emphasis clearly.

To complicate matters further, the thought with which we are working here has two kinds of chiasms operating synchronically. One is an organizational, or structural, chiasm. The other is an artistic or poetic chiasm. As we shall see, these two types of patterns work together, reinforcing each other and the point that is being made.

The organizational, or structural, chiasm can be discerned by looking at the various sections of the composition in terms of the content. In 2:13-17 there is a general injunction to everyone in the community to be subject to human institutions; then, in 2:18-20, a specific injunction to servants to be subject to their masters. In 2:21-24 there is a Christological hymn, which centers the chiasm. Then the repetition begins. In 3:1-6 there is the specific injunction to wives to be subject to their husbands. Then in 3:8ff there is again a general injunction to all not to return evil for evil which supplies the rationale for the whole series of injunctions.

The chiasm, therefore, is based upon the symmetry developed by juxtaposing a general injunction, a specific injunction, the hymn, a specific injunction and a general injunction.

The artistic, or poetic, chiasm can be discerned by looking at the Christological hymn which
forms the center of the organizational chiasm.
This hymn, which is set up as a poem in Nestle's
Greek text but not in the English, is composed of a
remarkable regular and symmetrical pattern of
lines. If you look at the passage as outlined
below, you will note that the line that begins the
poem and the line that ends the poem each have
eight syllables. You will also notice that the
syllabic pattern at the center of the piece is very
tight. An unusually short line, one with only six
syllables, is framed by two lines of twelve syllables which are in turn framed by two lines of
fourteen syllables:

(8)     a 21 εἰς τοῦτο γὰρ ἐκλήθητε,
        b ὅτι καὶ Χριστὸς ἔπαθεν ὑπὲρ ὑμῶν
        c ὑμῖν ὑπολιμπάνων ὑπογραμμὸν
        d ἵνα ἐπακολουθήσητε τοῖς ἴχνεσιν αὐτοῦ,
        a 22 ὃς ἁμαρτίαν οὐκ ἐποίησεν
(14)    b οὐδὲ εὑρέθη δόλος ἐν τῷ στόματι αὐτοῦ,
(12)    a 23 ὃς λοιδορούμενος οὐκ ἀντελοιδόρει,
 (6)    b πάσχων οὐκ ἠπείλει,
(12)    c παρεδίδου δὲ τῷ κρίνοντι δικαίως·
(14)    a 24 ὃς τὰς ἁμαρτίας ἡμῶν αὐτὸς ἀνήνεγκεν
        b ἐν τῷ σώματι αὐτοῦ ἐπὶ τὸ ξύλον,
        c ἵνα ταῖς ἁμαρτίαις ἀπογενόμενοι
        d τῇ δικαιοσύνῃ ζήσωμεν,
(8)     e οὗ τῷ μώλωπι ἰάθητε.


        a 21 For to this you have been called
        b because Christ also suffered for you
        c leaving you an example
        d that you should follow in his steps.
        a 22 He committed no sin
        b no guile was found on his lips.
        a 23 When he was reviled, he did not revile in return
        b when he suffered he did not threaten
        c but he trusted to him who judges justly.
        a 24 He himself bore our sins
        b in his body on the tree
        c that we might die to sin
        d and live to righteousness.
        e By his wounds you have been healed.

In  addition  to the syllabic regularity, there
are some striking resonances in both the syntax and
the  semantics of the poem.  The last phrase of the
first  line  is  an  aorist passive, eklethete (you
have been called) which the last phrase of the last
line  is  another aorist passive, iathete (you have
been  healed).    Moreover, the fourth line and the
third  line  from the end resemble each other.  21d
is  a  hina clause, "in order that you might follow
in his steps" while 24c is another hina clause, "in
order that we might die to sin."  The similarity of
phraseology and the relative symmetry of the place-
ment  of  the two expressions should at least raise
the  question  as  to whether the two ideas are not
being  equated  in  the  vernacular of 1 Peter.  We
might  posit  that  both  clauses state responses
desired of the believers--"that you might follow in
his footprints,"--"that having died to sin we might
live  for justice."  This arrangement at least suggests that the two lines might serve to explain one
another.    In  other  words, the terms of the hymn
suggest  that  following  in  the footprints of the
Christ  might involve dying to sin and, conversely,
that dying to sin might involve actually walking in
the way of Christ.
    Another  pair  of phrases that we should compare
are  the  second  line, 21b, "that Christ also suffered  (var. died) for us," and 24d, "that we might
live."  These two phrases form a semantic balance--
he  suffered  or,  as the variant supplies, he died
(21b) that we might live (24d).
    Having  dealt  with the outermost components of
the chiastic hymn, let us turn our attention to the
center  and, in this case, the major concern of the
poet.    We  might begin by looking at 22b and 24b.
The phrases are, respectively, "nor was there guile
found  in his mouth" and "in his body on the tree."
While  both these phrases function primarily within
their  respective sentences, their visual and aural
symmetry  (en to stomati autou/en to somati autou)
mark  the  chiastic  intent of the piece by framing
the crucial point of the hymn.
    Finally,  it  is  at  that  center to which our
attention  is  gradually  being  drawn.  We observe
that  the  center  consists of the three hos clauses
and  that  the  two outside clauses of this unit of
three  exhibit  symmetry  in  the  use of hamartian

(22a) and hamartias (24a). These observations lead
me to believe that the central point of the hymn is
contained in 23, where, as we have already noted,
the syllabification is most tightly controlled in a
pattern of 12/6/12. These three lines, ["who being
cursed did not return a curse / suffering (paschon)
did not threaten / but yielded to the one who
judges justly" (dikaios)] as the central meaning of
the hymn refer, in this particular prose context,
back to the last usage of paschon, in 2:19, in connection with the behavior of slaves in relationship
to their masters. That this is, in fact, the
intention of the argument is strengthened by the
fact that the dikaios of 23c resonates with the
adikos of 19c. Thus the injunction to slaves to
submit to unjust masters and, thereby, to "do good"
is rooted in the example of Christ who did not
return a curse for a curse nor a threat for suffering. These actions of not-repaying-in-kind, in the
case of Christ as in the case of slaves, are
rendered meaningful by the appeal to a higher
order, by yielding present injustice to the one who
judges justly—an act accomplished precisely by not
returning in kind. In this sense, submission to
every human creation is an act performed by those
who are free with respect to these human institutions because they are, as Theou douloi (16c),
slaves of a higher order.

In summary, we might note that: 1) the
chiastic form of the hymn draws our attention
inward to the model of the Christ who does not
return evil for evil; and 2) the chiastic structure
of the surrounding material suggests that slaves
and wives are particular models of this Christ-type
and, therefore, serve as examples to the community.
Therefore, we can assume that the text is setting
up the relationships in something of the following
pattern:

| human institution | "master" | tormentors |
|---|---|---|
| community | slave | Christ |

| "husbands" | evil |
|---|---|
| wives | good |

I think we need to be careful at this point not
to oversimplify the text. The equations are not

simple correspondences. Rather the relationships
in the equations are being treated as in some
senses analogous. The subordination of Christ to
his tormentors is the model for slaves and women
who are models for the community.

Having looked at the way the injunctions to
slaves and wives are related to the theme of not
repaying in kind and how in their suffering submission the wives and slaves imitate Christ, let us
compare the injunction to youth in the second section. First of all we might note that whereas the
slaves and the wives received the primary exhortation in the previous injunctions, here the elder is
exhorted first. Secondly, Peter addresses the
elders as one of them and specifically as a co-
witness of the sufferings of Christ. Third, the
elders are specifically conjoined not to "lord it
over" the youth but to be examples to the flock.
(In the vernacular of 1 Peter, what could an "example" mean but a sufferer?) Fourth, while the youth
are conjoined to submit to the elders, this command
is not justified by an appeal to a Christological
hymn. Obeying those more experienced in the faith
makes sense to the author of 1 Peter, but it is not
couched either in the language of not repaying in
kind or in the language of missionary appeal.
Finally, the injunction is immediately and con-
clusively qualified by the mutuality of the command
to "clothe yourselves...with humility toward one
another."

These differences in the treatment of the
elder-youth pair from the treatment of the husband-
wife and master-slave pairings seem to be rather
marked and, I think, of some significance to feminist hermeneutics. Let me suggest some of the ways
these learnings may be significant:
    1. It seems clear that from the point of view
of the text, both slavery and patriarchy are
institutions which are beyond the control of the
community. The mention of bad masters and
unChristian husbands seem to indicate that slavery
and patriarchy are not divine institutions but one
of those "human institutions" which are problematic
for the community. Given those social realities,
the author is saying, the community has a somewhat
limited range of possible reactions. The option
the author is encouraging is that of not returning

evil for evil. By contrast, a limited and
qualified hierarchy based on religious maturity is
to be fostered within the church, but there is no
indication in the letter that the institutions of
slavery and patriarchy have any function within the
community itself.

2. The hardest question for feminist
hermeneutics is the question of appropriation. Is
the text useful for oppressed people--whether women
or those enslaved in other ways? That question is
and should be an ongoing one--one with which the
community of believers should continue to struggle.
There are only a few comments I can make toward
resolution of that question. First, the way the
text is structured precludes separating the issues
of slavery and women's subordination--simply
because the text treats them as parallel cases.
However we deal with these issues, we must deal
with them together--at least in light of this text.
Secondly, it seems to me that the ethic of not
returning evil for evil may imply a critique. If
the submission of slaves and women are seen in
relation to "returning good for evil," there is a
certain sense in which slavery and patriarchy are
being named as evil. Third, as David Schroeder has
suggested, in the first century culture of Asia
Minor, slaves and wives would have been expected
and required to adopt the religions of their
masters and their husbands. Let us not fail to see
that these injunctions to be submissive are given
within the context of the author's support for a
major insubordination on the part of slaves and
wives--that of choosing their own faith.

In conclusion, I think I would go this far:
while a case for wifely submission as well as for
slavery can be made from Scripture (as Willard
Swartley demonstrates in Slavery, Sabbath, War and
Women), I'm beginning to think that an argument for
the maintenance of these institutions cannot be
made from this text of 1 Peter.

# GOD AS FRIEND: JEPHTHAH'S DAUGHTER
## Judges 11:29-40

### Mary Schertz

In this study we will explore the third of the feminist uses of Scripture that Sakenfeld mentions: "Looking to texts about women to learn from the intersection of history and stories of ancient and modern women living in patriarchal cultures." Some of these ancient texts about women are both viable and valuable in the theological enterprise of contemporary women. Specifically, I suggest that the story of the daughter of Jephthah in Judges 11:29-40 can help us think about a contemporary model of God that has potential for modern women—a model of God as friend.

I will begin with some general comments about the model of God as friend and then focus more specifically in the text. I should also add that at the point at which we look at the text I will be theologizing upon, not exegeting the text. I will be relying for exegesis on Phyllis Trible's work in Texts of Terror.

### Constructing a Model

In the last chapter of Sallie McFague's Metaphorical Theology, we are introduced to a model of God as friend that originates in an ideal of friendship. She notes that:

By "friendship" we do not of course mean easy empathy for one's own kind to be found in clubs, secret societies, and unfortunately, churches all over the world. Genuine friendship does not negate differences but can thrive on them, as the old adage, "opposites attract," suggests. But even beyond the personal level, the ideal of friendship to the stranger, to the alien both as individual and as nation or culture, suggests a model. Like Dante's vision of the harmony in paradise where the saints hold hands and dance in a circle, the friendship model is one for the future on our increasingly small and beleaguered planet, where, if people do$_1$ not become friends, they will not survive.

Even in this brief sample, it is clear that construction from the ideal is not only useful and provocative but essential to the process of model-making. If we propose that the divine is like a friend, then both logic and piety demand that we think carefully and clearly about the constitution of the most profound realizations of that relationship.

While I appreciate the necessity of constructing a model from such an ideal, I would like to suggest that an additional, and complementary, approach is also needed. This alternative procedure may be designated as realistic rather than ideal and minimal rather than maximal. In other words, my first question is not: What characterizes profound friendship and how may we construct a model from those understandings? Rather, my first questions are: What elements are essential or basic to all sorts of friendships? What do we have to have, and how do we have to be, in order to build a friendship? And how, then, may we construct a model from those understandings?

Such an inquiry, I think, yields two points. The first is that friendship requires the proximity of two subjects, and the second is that friendship requires these two subjects to recognize each other as subjects. With respect to proximity, while there are special senses in which physical proximity may not be a necessary starting point for friendship--such as the friendships which can occur between pen pals or the "friendship" we may feel for a character in a favorite novel or the process by which we may name and utilize some figure as a "theological companion"--usual friendships begin when we share space with another person for shorter or longer periods of time. In addition, even the special types of friendship I mentioned commonly depend on some sort of physical proximity although that proximity may be limited to holding a book or telephone.

With respect to the recognition of each other as subject, I mean an understanding of the other as like the self in her or his possession of humanness and unlike the self in his or her possession of a variety of humanness. While most understandings of friendship would insist that such regard be qualified as positive regard in order for friendship to

occur, I am more interested in delimiting indifference or a view of the other subject as an object
or an appendage. While friendship may survive, and
even thrive, despite some antagonisms, indifference
or objectification are almost always fatal to such
a relationship.

This identification of the real and minimal
requirements for friendship matters to the construct of God as friend because we can thereby
identify both the ontological claim and the confessional claim upon which the construct is based.
The ontological claim is God's proximity or, in
more conventional theological language, God's
"presence." In accordance with metaphorical
theory, it probably behooves us to characterize
this as a "shy ontological claim"—encompassing,
even at this very basic level, the "it is" and "it
is not."[2] But, however "shy" the claim, it seems
important to note that we construct a model of a
God who relates to us as a mature, ideal friend
upon the ontological claim that God is <u>present</u>.

If, then, the claim that God is proximate, or
present, is the ontological claim that grounds an
understanding of God as friend, the process between
that ontological claim and the construction of a
model which incorporates our best insights as to
what constitutes profound friendship is the confessional claim that God is not only present, but is a
subject who regards us as subjects. While God's
presence could be, and has been, construed in many
ways, God as friend depends upon a particular
stance, an essential willingness to think about God
in personal ways, that can only be characterized as
a risk of faith.

Therefore the view of God as friend developed
in this project presupposes that the bases of
friendship are proximity and the recognition of
each other as subjects. From the perspective of
the constructive task, these real and minimal components become, respectively, the ontological and
confessional claims which provide the foundation
for and guide subsequent construction of God as
friend. With those methodological understandings
in mind, let us explore the model from the perspective of three specific theological issues.

Testing the Model
1.   A Theoretical Issue:   Considerations of Scripture and Tradition
     The issues of  Scripture and tradition may be
formulated in two questions:  1) What is the source
of  God  as  friend in Scripture and the tradition?
2)  How  much  does it matter?  Of these questions,
the second is more important than the first for the
simple reason that neither Scripture nor the tradition  are  rich resources for this particular model.
As  McFague says in Metaphorical Theology, the term
"friend" appears only "here and there in the Bible"
and  "sparingly"  in  the tradition.³  That paucity
forces  us to look more closely at the second question,  an issue which, I suggest, may be focused by
posing  two additional questions.  First, since the
model of God as friend is not a major one in Scripture  or  tradition,  how  may we determine whether
such  a  model  is an appropriate one with which to
suggest  the human/divine relationship intrinsic to
the  faith  emerging from these documents?  Second,
is  connecting  these new and alternative models of
God to the documents necessary for the type of constructive  task with which metaphorical theology is
engaged?  Since the answer to the first question is
dependent  upon the second, we might logically deal
first with the latter.
     Obviously,  the  priority  of  the  connections
between  alternative  models of God and traditional
theological  sources  such as sacred texts, creeds,
etc.  is  influenced  by  a wide variety of factors
such  as  the  religious  background and vocational
choices  of the interpreters.  Those considerations
aside,  however,  I  suggest that there are reasons
intrinsic to metaphorical theology itself that make
the answer to the question "yes."  The first reason
is  that  the  nature  of  metaphorical theology is
literary  and therefore rhetorical.  Although other
forms  of  theology  also  presume an audience, and
are, of course, also rhetorical to some extent, the
distinguishing  feature of metaphorical theology is
its interest in a rhetorical figure.  Consequently,
there  is less distance between this type of theology  and its audience than, for example, systematic
or process thought precisely because the communication  process  is part of its concern.  Taking into
account the semantic fields in which the audiences'

systems of belief are embedded is a persuasive tactic consonant with these interests in communication.

The second reason is also rhetorical, but it
is, in addition, more directly focused on the
operational attributes of a metaphor or model.
These types of language operate as the tension
created$_4$by comparing elements in different semantic
fields. If our everyday experience of friendship
provides one such semantic field, then logic indicates that Scripture and tradition belong to the
semantic field in which images of the divine are
embedded. So I conclude that the very strength of
metaphorical theology--its ability to see connections "of a tensive, discontinuous and surprising
nature"$_5$ is dependent upon an understanding of
Scripture and tradition as vital to the project.

If Scripture and tradition are thus necessary
to the imaginative construct of alternative models
of God because they constitute one of the semantic
fields being held in tension by the model, then how
does one manage such an integral comparison if, as
with God as friend, the model does not figure significantly in either? I suggest that the presence
or absence of a particular model in Scripture and
the tradition is less important than an evaluation
of whether the ontological and confessional claims
which form the bases of the construct are consonant. In the case of God as friend, these
bases--the presence of God and the concept of God
as a subject who recognizes persons as subjects--
are attested in a variety of ways in both Scripture
and tradition. Therefore, since this basic ground-
ing in the semantic field in which this particular
(Christian) religion signifies the divine is in
place, the theologian can, with confidence, construct a model of God as friend using both the concrete images which are available and developing
additional expressions of God as friend appropriate
to the ontological and confessional claims upon
which the model rests.

2. A Doctrinal Issue: Implications for Salvation
Having determined that God as friend is an
appropriate expression of the human/divine relationship intrinsic to the Christian faith, we can
begin to construct the model of God as friend by
considering one aspect of that construction--how

the model might shape an understanding of salvation.

In the context of Christianity, such an understanding depends to a large extent upon an understanding of Jesus as the redeeming figure. Therefore the first consideration is necessarily some consideration of the implications of God as friend for the doctrine of the person and work of Jesus. Both Moltmann's chapter in The Passion for Life and McFague's in Metaphorical Theology contain Christological sections. Moltmann cites two scriptural references to Jesus as friend--the Synoptic description of Jesus as "a glutton and a drunkard, a friend of tax collectors and sinners" (Luke 7:34 and Matthean parallel), and a description of the conversation in which Jesus invites the disciples to the kind of friendship that involves laying down one's life for the friend (John 15). Moltmann relates both of these examples of Jesus as friend to an inner motivation rooted in "joy in God and humanity." It is this "overflowing" and self-sacrificing joy that renders "dependent, obedient" relationships (such as servant-master: wife-husband: child-parent) void and, instead, invites friendship.[6]

McFague, using a broader range of Scriptural allusions, says that "Jesus, in his identification with the sufferings of others throughout his life and especially at his death, is a parable of God's friendship with us at the most profound level."[7]

In addition to those insights, the application[8] of an Anabaptist-Mennonite Christological outline to the model of Jesus as friend might indicate the following points. First, Jesus' friendship with the outcasts, his identification with those who suffer, grows out of another, primary relationship. Jesus is first and foremost God's friend. In this sense Jesus stands within a "friend of God" tradition that dates back to Abraham[9] and also serves as a prototype of the friendship with the divine to which disciples are called. If Jesus is God's friend then we might consider Jesus' ministry and death as illustrative of his loyalty to the purposes and intents of that friendship with God. Both the temptations and Jesus' prayer life provide examples of the very real struggles involved in putting the interest of one's friend above one's

self-interest. These are real struggles because
the priority of this friendship with God, in fact,
results in conflict--with the religious people of
his community, with the political powers that ruled
that community and even (first occasionally and
then with tragic finality) with the very community
he has himself called together to represent the new
reality. However, it is exactly at that point
where Jesus' friendship with God has cost him every
other friend he ever had--when even "the women who
had followed him from Galilee stood at a distance"
(Luke 23:49)--that Jesus best illustrates not only
the kind of friendship he has with God, but also
the kind of friendship God offers us. Because in
that extreme experience of isolation, that experience of utter lack of any friendship, at a time
when he thought that even God had deserted him,
Jesus remained loyal to God's purposes. He refused
to perpetuate the enmity, choosing instead to suffer and to forgive. In other words, Jesus remained
present: he did not flee suffering and he chose to
continue to regard his enemies as subjects even
though the personal cost proved ultimate.

If we thus understand Jesus' ministry and death
in the context of his friendship with God, the kind
of salvation implied by this understanding might be
characterized as acts of reconciliation. Living
lives reconciled to God, or being God's friends, is
not only something we are but also something we do.
In other words while we might be God's friends, and
thus "saved," we experience that redemption, we
work out that salvation, as we extend acts of
reconciliation. We are God's friends as we choose
to end cycles of enmity by offering God's
friendship instead of returning evil for evil.
Thus, it would seem to me, the kind of salvation
implied by the model of God as friend can not by
nature be limited to personal salvation but must
include a broad consideration of reconciliation--a
consideration as extended as the circumference of
existing enmities between individuals, between gen-
ders, races and classes of people, between humanity
and nature, and among the nations of the earth.

3.     An Experiential Issue: Applications for a
Nuclear Age

A third kind of test is a consideration of how
the model might speak to, and also from, our expe-

rience.  While there is a variety of ways to focus
these  questions  of  experience  in relation to the
model  of  God as friend, I suggest we focus on one
aspect  of  human  experience--our  experience  of
living  in  a world threatened by nuclear annihila-
tion.  I  suggest this focus on two counts.  Most
importantly,  the  issue  is  a pressing one in our
contemporary world.  Second, the sheer starkness of
the issue may prove illuminative in the development
and evaluation of the model of God as friend.

From[10] theological  studies  of  the  nuclear
issues,  we might posit three sorts of criteria by
which  to  evaluate  the  adequacy  of  alternative
models  of  God for our age.  These studies seem to
suggest that such a model should provide:  1) a way
to  think  about  the connectedness between God and
the  world;  2)  a  way  to  think  about  human
responsibility  in this situation of crisis; and 3)
a way to think about hope in the midst of the overwhelmingly  destructive  capacity  which has thrust
the crisis upon us.

While  the  God-world  connection  might be developed in relation to the friendship model by, for
example,  utilizing the insights of Native American
religions  or  those of feminist Goddess religions,
the  ontological  and confessional bases identified
seem  to  indicate  that other models might be more
immediately  available  for  this  consideration.
Therefore,  we  might concentrate on the latter two
issues--the  matters  of  human  responsibility and
hope.  These matters may be clarified by a text--
the  account  in Judges 11:29-40 of the daughter of
Jephthah  and  Phyllis  Trible's exposition of this
text.[11]  At least I want to suggest that Jephthah's
daughter provides a model of God as friend that can
be  genuinely  helpful  for a nuclear age.  In this
story  Jephthah,  an Israelite warrior, makes a vow
to  Yahweh  to  the effect that if he is victorious
over  the  Ammonites "whoever comes forth from the
doors  of  my  house to meet me, when I return victorious from the Ammonites, shall be the Lord's and
I  will  offer him up for a burnt offering" (Judges
11:31,  RSV).  Subsequently,  Jephthah wins his
battle  and returns home a war hero.  However, when
his  only  heir, a daughter, comes dancing to greet
him,  it  becomes  clear  that  his  hasty vow has
precipitated a tragedy.

In order to understand how this tale of an
ancient catastrophe speaks to our age of nuclear
readiness we might begin by pointing out some
similarities between the text as interpreted by
Trible and our contemporary situation. Trible
characterizes the setting as one in which public
and private events are interlocked.[12] In Jephthah's bargain with the divine, which Trible notes
as an unnecessary bargain since Yahweh's compassion
is already assured,[13] he pledges his private well-
being for a national and military goal. Not only
does he thus indicate his willingness to sacrifice
the private for the public, but he is willing to do
so without considering the ramifications of that
willingness and without considering the real price
of his negotiation with the divine for the outcome
of his battle. As a result of the vow that Trible
defines as an "act of unfaithfulness" emerging from
Jephthah's "desires to bind God rather than to
embrace the gift of the spirit,"[14] Jephthah in fact
sets in motion the circumstances that will engulf
both him and his daughter in a particular kind of
death. As Trible notes:

..this particular death defies all the
categories of the natural and the expected.
First, it is premature; life ends before
its potential has unfolded. If King
Hezekiah could weep bitterly that "in the
noontide" of his days he must depart (Isa.
38:3, 10), how much more this child must
lament in the morning of her life. Second,
her death is to be violent. Death by fire
is bitter death, and more bitter still when
its author is her very own father. Third,
her death will leave no heirs because she
is a virgin. What alone designated fulfillment for every Hebrew woman, the bearing of children, will never be hers to know
(cf. 1 Sam. 1:1-20). Truly, with no child
to succeed her, she may be numbered among
the unremembered, those "who have perished
as though they had not lived" (Sirach
44:9). Premature, violent, without an
heir: all the marks of unnatural death
befall this young woman, and she is not
even spared the knowledge of them. Hers is

premeditated   death,   a   sentence of murder
passed   upon   an   innocent   victim because of
the   faithless   vow   uttered   by her foolish
father.[15]

The   parallels between the death awaiting Jephthah's   daughter   and the nuclear death awaiting us
and our planet are striking:
    --Nuclear   death also defies all the categories
within   which   the   human   community has heretofore
rendered death significant.
    --This death is also a violent death by fire.
    --This   death   is   authored   by   those among us
charged with responsibility for our common welfare.
    --This   death, too, permits no heirs, no future
generations.
    --This   death threatens us too with being "num-
bered among the unremembered."
    --Like   Jephthah's   daughter,   we   also are not
spared a fullsome knowledge of this empty death.
    With   these   parallels   in   mind,   and with the
criteria having to do with human responsibility and
hope   in   mind,   let me suggest two ways the actions
and responses of the daughter of Jephthah may guide
our   thinking   about   God as friend in this nuclear
age.
    1.   Trible notes that when she hears the awful,
condemning   words of her father, the daughter "does
not   seek   to   deny or defy them, nor does she show
anger   or   depression.   No sentiment of self-pity
passes   her lips; instead, she feels for her father
the   compassion that he has not extended to her."[16]
Notice   that   even as the desperation of her plight
becomes   clear to her, even as she becomes achingly
aware   that   her father has effectively reduced her
to an object with which to barter for the spoils of
war,   Jephthah's   daughter   continues to regard her
father as a subject, as fully human.   She continues
to respect his freedom to make decisions, even when
those   decisions   are not only self-destructive but
destructive of their entire lineage.
    In light of this woman's response to her situa-
tion,   one   important   understanding   that God as
friend   contributes to theological understanding in
a   nuclear   age   is   that God's nature as subject
regarding   us   as   co-subjects   is   self-limiting.
Within   the   framework   of   Her friendship with Her

world, human freedom is a gift God will not rescind
even if, as with the case of Jephthah's daughter,
Her own body (in the sense in which Grace Jantzen
defines the term "God's body"[17]) is at stake. If
God will not violate our status as friends, even
when the fate of the earth is at stake, then it
seems we can do little other than acknowledge that
the role we have assumed in this haunting drama is
Jephthah's role. We too have bartered the wellbe-
ing of those we love as well as our entire lineage
for the spoils of war. If God is friend, we can
hardly escape the recognition that in creating this
unholy bargain we have seriously violated the terms
of that friendship. We can hardly escape the
knowledge that if the bargain is to be rendered
void (so that we may continue to live) we will need
to repent and redirect our lives.

2.    If the model of God as friend provides a
way to think about human responsibility in the
nuclear age, the next, and more difficult question,
is whether the model provides a way to think about
hope. Although the story of Jephthah's daughter is
certainly an unmitigated tragedy, I think it
nevertheless contains the key to that hope. Trible
notes that "the victim assumes responsibility, not
for blame but for integrity."[18]  The daughter separates herself from her father and seeks her friends
in order to go with them and "to wander upon the
hills and lament her virginity." And even though
the action does not stay the outcome, the daughter
of Jephthah imparts her own meaning to the meaninglessness by:  1) naming the unholiness of the
bargain;  2) separating herself from the unholiness
without denigrating or objectifying the perpetuator
of the unholiness; 3) ending her isolation, choosing to share her grief and terror with her friends
on the mountain.

Perhaps, in this nuclear age, this story and,
more broadly, the model of God as friend helps us
define a special kind of hope. I suggest that this
hope is not the large kind of hope we may want to
provide.  It may not be the kind of hope other
theologies offer and it may not be the kind of hope
other models can provide. I think, however, that
while the hope consonant with God as friend may be
a small hope, it is nevertheless a real hope. This
hope involves a recognition that human being

partakes in part of both Jephthah and Jephthah's
daughter.  Where we have violated God's friendship
we  need to accept blame and find constructive ways
to  repent.  Where we have been victimized we need
to  accept  responsibility  for  our integrity.  In
both cases we need to end our isolation and reclaim
our  rightful  status as friends in the presence of
the  God  who is our friend.  These actions do not,
of  course,  guarantee  the  outcome  and there may
indeed  be  no  one  left  to mourn us.  But at any
rate, we do possess the present, a time in which we
may  understand  God  as  present, as a subject who
regards  us as subject, as our friend.  We need not
live in isolation.

## Notes

1. Sallie McFague, Metaphorical Theology: Models of God in Religious Language (Philadelphia: Fortress Press, 1981), 179.
2. Ian G. Barbour, Myths, Models and Paradigms (New York: Harper and Row, 1976), 14.
3. McFague, Metaphorical Theology, 178.
4. Ibid., 37ff.
5. Ibid., 14.
6. Jürgen Moltmann, The Passion for Life: A Messianic Life Style (Philadelphia: Fortress Press, 1977), 57.
7. McFague, Metaphorical Theology, 180.
8. The outline developed by Marlin E. Miller for a class entitled "Systematic Theology from a Believers' Church Perspective" (Associated Mennonite Biblical Seminaries, Elkhart, IN, Fall, 1982), might be considered a representative Anabaptist-Mennonite view. According to this view, an adequate Christology includes the following topics: 1) Jesus as Jesus of Nazareth or, in other words, the figure concretized by the texts; 2) Jesus and the Kingdom of God; 3) Jesus' faith and discipleship; 4) Jesus' conflicts in life; 5) Death by crucifixion; 6) Resurrection and glorification; 7) The Person of Christ.

As is clear from the Moltmann and McFague formulations as well as mine, the friend model is most illuminative and least "forced" with respect to those aspects of Christology which explain Jesus' vocation in life and the death which resulted from the practice of that vocation (points 1-5). While a thorough exploration of the significance of these particular intersections is beyond the scope of this paper, we might simply note that the pertinence between metaphorical and systematic theologies is sufficiently mutually suggestive and explanatory so as to merit careful study of a variety of concrete models in relation to appropriate doctrinal topics.

9. McFague, Metaphorical Theology, 178.
10. Two examples of studies which incorporate a consciousness of the nuclear situation are: Harold K. Schilling, "The Whole Earth is the Lord's: Toward a Holistic Ethic," in Earth Might Be Fair: Reflections on Ethics, Religion and Ecology, ed. Ian G. Barbour (Englewood Cliffs, New Jer-

sey:      Prentice-Hall, 1977), 100-122; and Dorothee
Soelle with Shirley A. Cloyes, To Work and to Love:
A    Theology  of  Creation (Philadelphia, Fortress
Press, 1984).

    11.  Phyllis Trible, "The Daughter of Jephthah:
An   Inhuman   Sacrifice,"  in  Texts  of  Terror:
Literary-Feminist Readings of Biblical Narratives
(Philadelphia:   Fortress Press, 1981), 93-116.

    12.  Ibid., 93.
    13.  Ibid., 97.
    14.  Ibid.
    15.  Ibid., 104.
    16.  Ibid., 102.

    17.  Grace   Jantzen's  God's World, God's Body
(Philadelphia:    Westminster  Press,  1984)  is an
extensive  elaboration  of  a  doctrine of the God-
world  relationship  based  on  a metaphoric understanding of the world as the body of God.

    18.  Trible, Texts of Terror, 103.

# IS GOD THE FRIEND OF SLAVES AND WIVES?

## Ben C. Ollenburger

My task is to respond to the essays in this volume by David Schroeder and Mary Schertz. A response would be uninteresting were it merely to report agreement. Besides, no one would be interested to know that I agree with the work of two New Testament scholars. My hope is to engender discussion, and that is more fruitfully done by taking issue than by offering applause. Thus, the tone of this response will sometimes be more critical than would be either necessary or warranted were I simply passing judgment on the quality of the essays. It is appropriate, however, to thank the authors for their work, which is both valuable and provocative. My response will be directed first to the essays of Schroeder and Schertz on the Haustafel, and then to Schertz's essay on Judges 11:29-40. I will make no comment on her study of Luke 19-21, but I hope it will be read.

## I. Schroeder and Schertz on the Haustafel

It is always instructive to have interpreters work on the same text from different perspectives, as Schroeder and Schertz have done on 1 Peter. I will take advantage of this happy circumstance by considering Schroeder's essay alongside Schertz's, pointing to the differences in method, the agreement in conclusions, and raising some issues. I will not quibble about whether other methods could or should have been used and will merely assume that Schroeder has done a good job of historical criticism and Schertz of rhetorical criticism. My interest is in how they use their respective methods, and in whether their use of these methods justifies the conclusions they draw.

In their readings of 1 Peter, Schroeder and Schertz confront the same problem: the apparently non-egalitarian and anti-feminist nature of the Haustafel or station code in 1 Peter 2 and 3.[1] Furthermore, both of them pursue the same goal: to disarm the text of its offensive possibilities by proposing interpretations in which the text supports, rather than opposes, those positions we have come to hold on the questions it addresses. The implicit or explicit goal is, in other words, to

show how that according to a new and proper reading, the text does not say what it eems to say.
However, this goal is pursued in different ways,
according to different strategies, and hence by
different methods.

Schroeder's account is a historical one. He
seeks to locate 1 Peter and the Haustafel within a
social and historical context. The context he
proposes is one in which Gentile converts to
Christianity were faced with the challenge of
remaining faithful to Christ in "stations" that
they would be unable to change. While they could
not change these stations, Christians were to take
their moral bearings not from them, but from
Christ; they were to remain in their stations and
submit to their superiors while maintaining ulti-
imate allegiance to Christ alone. Thus, the
Haustafel does not reinforce the status quo, but
subverts it in an egalitarian direction by addressing women and slaves, for example, as responsible
agents according to the ideal of Galatians 3:28.
Schroeder's explanation of the Haustafel in 1 Peter
is, then, by reference to other parts of the book
and to the historical and social context in which
he assumes it was located.

Schertz's account is a literary one. Except
for a reference to David Schroeder's paper, she
makes no mention of the historical and social context; it plays no role in her account. Instead,
she locates the specific elements of the text in
relation to its literary and syntactic structure.
She finds a larger chiasm in 2:13-3:8ff., centering
on the poem in 2:21-23, and a smaller chiasm within
the poem itself, centering on 2:23. The effect of
this structure, Schertz concludes, is to portray
the submission of slaves to their masters, and
wives to their (non-Christian?) husbands, as
modelled on the non-resistant Christ, who did not
return evil for evil. Thus, Schertz finds at least
an implicit critique of slavery and patriarchy in 1
Peter. Both are analogous to the evil that is
beyond the control of Christians, to which they
submit, and which thereby constitute a test of
faithfulness.

Despite their different methods, Schroeder and
Schertz reach strikingly similar conclusions. Each
of them has disarmed an offensive text, transform-

ing it from socially conservative into radically
(if implicitly) subversive. They have accomplished
this disarmament in the same general way, despite
the obvious differences in particulars. That is,
each of them establishes a background against which
to read the text; this background then sets the
terms of interpretation. For Schroeder, the background is the structure of the "house" in 1 Peter's
Graeco-Roman context, while for Schertz the background is the chiastic structure of the text
itself. For Schroeder, it is crucial to establish
the date, origin, and purpose of the Haustafel from
the outset; he speaks here of "assumptions." For
Schertz, these matters are strictly secondary; the
question of purpose arises only subsequent to a
close reading of the text. Schroeder does make
reference to the literary context of the Haustafel,
but gives no attention to the rhetorical features
that are central to Schertz's approach. In sum,
background is crucial to both of them, but each
appeals to a different kind of background.

Does method make an important difference? In
this case, apparently not. It is not obvious that
Schroeder and Schertz would disagree with each
other. Neither paper is hostile to the approach of
the other. Schroeder could have incorporated a
discussion of chiasm--he does make modest comments
about structure--and Schertz could have discussed 1
Peter's historical and social context, without dis-
turbing the argument of either paper. Such a combination of approaches may have produced a stronger
argument than either Schroeder or Schertz has
mounted independently; nonetheless, each paper
achieved its goal. Schroeder wanted to argue that
1 Peter is egalitarian and not status quo (as in
his title), while Schertz wanted to pursue a feminist strategy of counteracting "famous texts used
'against' women" (p. 76). Schertz could have
achieved her goal using Schroeder's method, and the
reverse is also true.

The central question in this case is not
whether historical readings or rhetorical ones are
better, though that question can be raised; [4]
rather, the central question here is whether the
background constructed on the basis of their
respective methods has been used by Schroeder and
Schertz to efface the specific texts in question.

Schroeder proposes a historical background
against which the Haustafel in 1 Peter is seen to
be egalitarian.[5] While slaves and wives are powerless to alter the institutions of slavery and
patriarchy, their faithfulness subverts those very
institutions and gives them a status as Christians
equal to masters and husbands. I will not contest
that 1 Peter views these institutions as unchangeable. But does the book view that situation as
lamentable? Does it, in other words, view slavery
and patriarchy to be incompatible with the Gospel?

1 Peter's exhortation to slaves is indeed com-
bined with a hymn on the nonresistant suffering of
Christ, but the text (2:18-25) does not compare
Christ's suffering with that of slaves generally.
It does not say that slavery should be viewed as a
form of suffering comparable to Christ's; rather,
it says that when slaves suffer patiently at the
hands of overbearing masters while "doing right"
they have God's approval, based on the pattern of
Christ's suffering. This is not a reproach of the
master-slave relationship but of its abuse, and
that only implicitly. That 1 Peter recognizes the
possibility of slavery's abuse is testimony that it
does not view it as evil in itself.

Similarly with respect to wives, 1 Peter does
indeed envision the possibility that submission may
lead to the conversion of husbands, some of whom
are apparently not believers (3:1). Still, wifely
submission seems to be valued in its own right:
God appreciates a gentle and quiet spirit (3:4),
and holy women of old were submissive to their husbands, Sarah even calling Abraham "lord" (3:5-6).
There is no suggestion in this text that patriarchy
is one of those things that wives must unfortunately suffer because they are powerless to change it.
To the contrary, it was modeled by the first
patriarch and his wife. Furthermore, the exhortation that follows in 3:7 is certainly to Christian
husbands; taken together with 3:1-6, it suggests
that 1 Peter is also addressing Christian wives and
husbands, rather than advocating only tactical submission to those wives caught up in an unchangeable
but lamentable pagan institution.

The evidence is sufficient, I suggest, at least
to raise the question whether Schroeder's historical method and his specific contextual assumptions

more nearly obscure the Haustafel texts than
explain them.   The background that he constructs
makes it more difficult, rather than easier, to
account for specific features of the text: for
example, its failure to raise a single critical
question of either slavery or patriarchy, or to
hint at their provisional, contextual status.   The
exhortation to "do right," to which Schroeder draws
frequent attention, seems to indicate the intrinsic
rightness of subordination to emperors (2:13-15),
masters (2:18-20), and husbands (3:1, 5).

The lesson will be the same with respect to
Schertz's essay.   Her rhetorical analysis clearly
shows the theological scaffolding of this section
of 1 Peter, centered on the nonresistant suffering
of Christ (2:23).   But the specific texts themselves, 2:18-20 and 3:1-6, do not claim that either
slaves or wives suffer by virtue of their institu-
tionally required or theologically motivated submission to something provisional and evil.   It is
the entire community, living under imperial power--
slaves, wives, and husbands--who are exhorted not
to return evil for evil (3:8).   Thus, the analogies
Schertz sets up (p. 80) seem to require modifica-
tion.   Rather than:

| human institution | "master" | tormentors |
|---|---|---|
| community | slave | Christ |

| "husbands" | evil |
|---|---|
| wives | good |

the analogies can be simplified as follows:

| overbearing masters | tormentors | evil |
|---|---|---|
| good slaves | Christ | good |

The text does not suggest that the imperial
government is evil or something to be suffered
(2:13-15), nor does it suggest that slavery and
patriarchy are evil.   Injustice is suffered not by
virtue of these institutions, claims 1 Peter, but
by virtue of their abuse--at least in the case of
slavery.   The text does not speak of institutional
injustice in relation to the empire, slavery, or
patriarchy.   It does speak of "various trials"
(1:6), evil and reviling (3:9), suffering on behalf
of righteousness (3:14), suffering in the flesh
(4:1), and suffering in the fiery ordeal that

befalls faithful Christians (4:12ff.). In none of
these passages is suffering associated with a
specific institution; all of them depict suffering
as an expected part of Christian faithfulness in a
world that pursues the fleshly passions and the
evil that Christians are to foreswear. Only in
reference to overbearing masters is suffering tied
to the perversion of an institution, against which
no special protest is raised or assumed. There is
indeed a relation between "every human creation" in
2:13 and God the "faithful Creator" in 4:19, as
Schertz notes; however, 1 Peter does not say that
every human creation ("institution") is subject to
the Creator, but that both the governors and the
Creator serve as motivations for Christians to "do
right." The text gives no hint that the right-
doing which governors are sent by the emperor to
praise (2:14) has a content at odds with the right-
doing that God now enjoins on the community.

I suggest, then, that the specific texts in
question continue to resist the efforts at disarmament that Schroeder and Schertz practice. Reading
them against an egalitarian or nonresistant background does make them more congenial to our interests, but only by effacing their specificity. Once
the controversial texts are themselves brought back
into the foreground, however, the proposed solutions seem ephemeral. Both Schroeder and Schertz
assume that the problems posed by these texts can
be resolved by showing that they do not say what
they seem to say. Both appeal to better data or
more careful analysis to show that "Slaves be submissive to your masters with all respect" is
really--given the proper method and the proper
background--subversive, egalitarian, and insubor-
dinate. It continues to seem quite otherwise.

This is not to suggest, on the other hand, that
we are bound to argue for slavery and patriarchy
because 1 Peter assumes both their unchangeable
existence and their legitimacy. It is to suggest
that a critique of those institutions and practices
based on 1 Peter will likely have to face squarely
the fact that chapters 2 and 3 make no criticisms
of them. The question, then, is whether there are,
within 1 Peter itself, theological resources for
formulating a critique of slavery and patriarchy,
and for repudiating both of them, and whether the

theological basis on which 1 Peter itself counsels
submission permits us and even requires us to
counsel something quite different. This is not a
question of method. I am not now criticizing the
way in which Schroeder and Schertz have practiced
their methods, nor do I have another one to propose
in their place. Insofar as I have a criticism to
make, it is only that Schroeder and Schertz have
required too much of their historical and rhetorical methods, asking them to solve what is at root a
theological problem.[6]

Does 1 Peter offer us the theological resources
for criticizing what it accepts? Indeed so, and
both Schroeder and Schertz point to them. For
example, Schroeder notes 1 Peter's own claims that
the overriding moral responsibility of Christians
consists in obedience to Christ (1 Peter 1:1, 14,
22), and that living according to the will of God
requires that former practices be abandoned (2:1-3;
4:2).[7] Furthermore, slaves and wives are included
in 1 Peter among those called "joint heirs of the
grace of life" (3:7). When these texts are read
from the perspective of the theological argument of
2:13-3:12, which Schertz describes extensively, we
have resources for constructing a theologically
grounded criticism and repudiation of slavery and
patriarchy, as well as much else.

1 Peter itself does not offer such a criticism,
of course, and the reasons it does not may be something like those cited by Schroeder (pp. 58-60).
The author of 1 Peter may have seen no choice for
Christian wives to be anything other than subject
to non-Christian husbands, and slaves to non-
Christian masters. And, it may not have occurred
to the author that slavery and patriarchy are practices inimical to the will of God as revealed in
the hymn of 2:21-24, or that obedience to the
Christ there depicted is not compatible with
institutions which implicitly deny that we are all
of us joint heirs of the grace of life. That 1
Peter did not draw these conclusions is historically interesting, but it seems to me futile to
argue by methodological appeal to some background
that, in fact, it did--that if we read the text
with proper historical assumptions or proper
rhetorical analysis, 1 Peter and its Haustafel are
egalitarian. They are probably not, but if we are

to be authentically biblical in our own faith and
practice, having read both 1 Peter and the rest of
the Bible, perhaps we must be.

To say this is not to warrant anachronistic
criticisms of 1 Peter, as if its author lives in
our day and spoke our language, nor is it to deny
that there may be times and places where and when
Christians must bear witness within institutions
that they are temporarily powerless to change--
perhaps even the church. It is merely to say that
1 Peter gives no explicit indication that it
regards slavery and patriarchy to be either temporary or inherently evil, and that--based in part
on what 1 Peter does say explicitly--we must say
something quite different about those institutions.

## II.  Schertz on Judges 11:29-40

Prior to considering Judges 11:29-40, the story
of Jephthah's daughter, Mary Schertz appeals to
metaphorical theology in arguing for a model of God
as friend. Her definition of friendship is minimalist:   it requires only two people in proximity
who regard each other as subjects. This definition
comports with a model of God that rests on an
ontological basis, that God is present, and a confessional basis, that God is a subject who regards
us as subjects. While our talk of friendship
derives from the "semantic field" of everyday experience, our talk of God derives from the semantic
field constituted by Scripture and tradition.
Given metaphorical theology's interest in communication and suasion, it appeals to Scripture as
a "persuasive tactic," thus bringing experience and
confessional tradition into a tensive relation.

There is a great deal here that I do not understand.   Why is the claim that God is present said
to be "ontological," while the claim that God is
subject-regarding said to be "confessional?" The
claims appear to be identical in both logic and
grammar.   I am unclear how this combination of
ontology and confession is related to the definition of friendship, or how the minimalist definitions of God and friend authorize the theologian to
construct a model of God as friend. How can we
speak of "everyday experience" as a semantic field,
and how is it that "logic indicates" that Scripture
and tradition constitute another semantic field?

Finally, can Christian theology be satisfied with
the arguments Schertz cites in favor of taking
Scripture and tradition into account in "constructive theology," since these arguments are rooted in
rhetorical strategy rather than in the identity of
Christian faith or its content?

My response to this essay will address
Schertz's methodological argument, as I have tried
to understand it, and her reading of Judges 11:29-
40.

Fundamental questions must be raised, it seems
to me, with respect to Schertz's comments about
ontology and confession. To the extent that I have
understood her, she means to say that ontological
claims about God, including the claim that God is
present, are made on the basis of sources other
than specifically Christian confession. In that
case, the confessional claim that God is subject-
regarding is a particular qualification of what we
can say about God's being non-confessionally.[11]
There is no harm in talking in terms of the ontology implicit in a Christian doctrine of God, if it
is not taken too seriously, but there is con-
siderable danger in regarding what we confess to be
a regional or sectarian qualification of (or addition to) a notion of the divine more universally
known. Ontology and confession need not have the
same deity as their subject. Schertz may be well
aware of the danger, but her distinction between
ontology and confession raises its spector, as does
her suggestion that "the God-world connection might
be developed... utilizing the insights of Native
American religions or those of feminist Goddess
religions" (p. 90).

This latter comment also provokes a question
about her notion of "metaphorical theology." Her
reason for utilizing Christian tradition rather
than Native American and Goddess religions to construct a connection between God and the world is
not one of principle; rather, it is that "other
models might be more immediately available" (p.
90). From what is said about metaphorical theology
earlier, I take it that "more immediately available" here means that appeal to Scripture would be
a better "persuasive tactic" (p. 87) in communicat-
ing with her audience (Mennonite feminist theologians) than would be an appeal to other religious

traditions.   As Schertz seems to define it, metaphorical theology chooses to appeal to Christian
tradition,  to  Christian  confession and to Scripture,  because that strategy will be most effective
in  persuading  Christians  to  adopt new models of
God.[12]    Theology always tried to be persuasive, and
is often polemical, but can its appeal to Scripture
be  merely tactical?  If it is merely a "persuasive
tactic,"  then  the  warning in the above paragraph
must be stressed with additional vigor.

      To  the  extent  that  I  have  understood her,
Schertz  argues  that God as friend is a model that
we  are  authorized  to  construct.    But I do not
believe  that she has made her case.  She bases her
argument  on  a  minimal definition of "friend," as
one  who  is  present and subject-regarding.  Given
her  definition  of  God on ontological and confessional  bases,  as  present  and subject-regarding,
there  is  a  natural  fitness  between her minimal
definition  of  friendship  and her equally minimal
definition  of  God.    Presumably, that is why the
definition of friendship needs to be minimal.  This
certainly  suffices as an argument for the abstract
possibility  of  "God as friend," assuming Schertz's
methodological  discussion,  but it is insufficient
as an argument for its adequacy or appropriateness.
It  offers  us  no  criteria  for determining which
metaphors  or models of presence and subject-regard
we must reject.[13]

      In other words, the way in which Schertz frames
her  argument  leaves  entirely open whether we may
appropriately  think  and  speak  of God as friend,
mother  (parent,  father,  sister, brother, brother-
in-law,  aunt), teacher (student, dean), therapist,
employer  (employee)  pastor  (parishioner),  col-
league,  nurse,  governor,  associate, confederate,
co-conspirator,  collaborator,  partner, liberator,
defender,  king,  and so forth.  All of these are or
should  be  present  to,  and properly regard their
correlatives  as  subjects  and  not as objects or
appendages.    The possibility is then open for them
to  function as metaphors or models of God.  What is
needed  is  an argument for the appropriateness and
adequacy of these or other images, and I do not see
that  Schertz  can  provide such an argument on the
terms that she spells out.

      Schertz  concludes  with a reading of the story

of Jephthah's daughter (Judges 11:29-40). My comments on her reading will be brief. She proposes that "Jephthah's daughter provides a model of God as friend that can be genuinely helpful for a nuclear age," and instructive for thinking about human responsibility and hope (p. 93). But I do not understand how this reading of the Jephthah's daughter story is to be connected with the earlier argument about God as friend. What authorizes us to construct from the enacted character of Jephthah's daughter a model of God? In the first place, there is no indication that her portrayal functions this way within the narrative. In the second place, even if we used the narrative for this purpose, would we want to speak of her actions toward either her father or God as those of a friend? Would we want to think of God in ways that her character embodies?

That is, even if we were to say that any character narratively portrayed in Scripture may serve as a source for our thought and speech about God, even if the narrative itself makes no such suggestions, and even if God is otherwise present in the narrative as an actor, I do not understand why we should want to orient our thought and speech about God on the character of Jephthah's daughter. Granted that her oppression and her fate is compellingly narrated, granted that her response to Jephthah's barbarous transaction is poignant, and granted that her humanity is in stark contrast to the machinations among Jephthah, God, and the Ammonites, yet her character and the narrative itself offer no attractive possibility for conceiving God or human responsibility and hope. Do we want to think of God as one who is bound by bargains struck between "friends," to which and to whom God can only be a victim—even a victim with remarkable humanity and integrity? Do we want to think of God as a friend so "self-limiting" in respect of us as subjects (p. 92) that, no matter how barbarous, murderous, and destructive of each other and of creation our actions and designs may be, God can say only "do to me according to what has gone forth from your mouth?" Does the action of Jephthah's daughter in withdrawing with friends for a time and then yielding to a fate she does not protest offer a serious model of human responsi-

bility and hope?    Schertz and Trible are quite
right;  Jephthah's daughter names the unholiness of
the  bargain, she separates herself from it without
denigrating its perpetrator, and  she shares her
grief with friends (p. 93).  This is a noble and
ennobling picture of response to a tragedy that has
not been avoided, but it offers us little help as a
portrayal  of what is required of us in the face of
potential tragedies, nuclear and otherwise.

If we are to speak of God as a friend, then we
must  speak  of  God  as  the friend whose wrath is
unfurled at  the  injustice  practiced against the
subjects of  God's own creation, as the friend who
judges those  who grind the faces of the poor, and
as  the  friend of sinners.  And if we sinners have
become friends of God, then we are required to lift
our  voice to this friend on behalf of victims like
Jephthah's  daughter  who  are slaughtered in God's
silence, and even--as  in  Judges  11:29-40--with
God's complicity.[14]

There  is  no reason why we should not speak of
God  also as our friend, and we require no particular  new  ontology to make such speech intelligible
and  appropriate.   But if it is really God of whom
we speak as friend, then this friend will also have
to  be  spoken of as Lord, and as the one who never
ceases  to  be  our  Lord and the Lord of creation.
And that is a decisive feature of God's grace, that
the one whom we address and must address as Lord is
also  the  one whom we are invited to call upon and
experience  as  friend, because  the  Lord  has
befriended us.

## Notes

1.   Schertz includes the exhortation to elders and youth in 1 Peter 5:1-5 within the Haustafel, considering them to be modifications of--or departures from--the exhortation to parents and children in Ephesians 6:1-4, and Colossians 3:20-21. She speaks of "the traditional three pairings" of master-slave, husband-wife, parent-child (see above, p. 75).   It seems to me, however, that 1 Peter 5:1-5 has nothing to do with a parent-child pairing.   The exhortation in 1 Peter is to elders (presbyteroi) and youth (neoteroi); in other words, it is a matter of ecclesiastical relationships, as she notes (p. 81). By contrast, in Ephesians and Colossians, the exhortation is to children (tekna) who are to obey their parents (goneis), and to fathers (pateres) who are not to provoke their children;   in other words, it is a matter of relationships within the biological family. The differences would seem to explain why 1 Peter does not treat the elder-youth relationship within the Haustafel, a fact on which Schertz places great stress.

2.   I am uncertain precisely what Schroeder means by "assumptions" in his essay (pp. 56-58). He uses the notion of Vorverständnis or preunderstanding to designate "those things that are assumed but not argued in the exegesis," such as the patriarchalism or political conservatism of most previous interpreters of 1 Peter. This is one kind of assumption, of a general sort and not specifically related to 1 Peter. On the other hand, he speaks in the same context of "assumptions" about the date, origin, and purpose of the Haustafel.   But an inquiry such as his, for which questions of date, origin, and purpose are both crucial and controverted, cannot assume answers to these questions without begging them. I take it that Schroeder wants to beg these technical questions temporarily in order to suggest the potentially controversial nature of more general assumptions.

3.   This is no criticism, of course. Methods can be conceived both as ways of finding new or different things in a text and as various ways of defending what we claim to find. Schroeder and

Schertz find the same thing in 1 Peter, but defend
their discovery in different ways.

4. No one kind of interpretation, or way of
reading the text, can be declared to be inherently
the best. There is a healthy kind of relativity to
interpretation. See Jeffrey Stout, "The Relativity
of Interpretation," The Monist 69 (1986) 103-17;
cf. Wayne C. Booth, Critical Understanding: The
Powers and Limits of Pluralism (Chicago: U. of
Chicago, 1979), especially pp. 235-56.

5. This is perhaps the only option when historical inquiry is meant to settle theological or
hermeneutical questions. In other words, if the
justification of our egalitarian commitments
depends on the author of 1 Peter having had the
same commitments, then it will be a matter of
theological urgency to show that he (presuming the
author to have been a man) actually had them. We
may sometimes want to argue that way, and may sometimes need to, but the conclusions of such arguments are always precarious, tentative, and subject
to challenge by someone who discovers a new text,
reads another language, or went to a different
graduate school.

6. See John Barton, Reading the Old Testament:
Method in Biblical Study (Philadelphia: Westminster, 1984) 204-297. I agree with Barton's
point that biblical criticism asks too much of its
"methods," even though his point and mine are somewhat different, and even though I disagree with
many of the observations he makes in reaching his
conclusion. What I will go on to propose in this
response is something like what has been called
"Sachkritik." A translation of that term would
serve no purpose; in any event, it is not another
method.

7. Schroeder, p. 60. Schroeder goes on
immediately to say that "The will of God with
respect to basic social responsibility" was spelled
out for new Gentile Christians "in the Haustafel."
How would this differ from their past practice?
The conversion of slaves and wives may have been
potentially subversive, but does not 1 Peter seem
precisely to temper this potential?

8. Perhaps Schertz means something like the
following. To make an ontological claim about God
is to attempt to think the being of God, and to

think the being of God is necessarily to think of God as present. The mode of God's being, as subject-regarding, is given in our confession. Hence, to think of God is to think of the divine as present and as subject-regarding, which is also the way we think of friendship. There is thus a certain fit between God and friendship, or the way God is and the way friends are, and metaphorical theology wants to exploit this fitness to persuade Christians to think and speak of God as friend.

9. Schertz says that the confessional claim that God is subject-regarding (a subject who regards us as subjects) is "the process between" the ontological claim of God's presence and the construction of a model based on our understanding of friendship (p. 85). I do not understand how one kind of claim can be a "process between" another kind of claim and the construction of a model.

10. A semantic field is usually thought to comprise lexical items within a given range of reference or denotation. It is difficult to comprehend what might be meant by the claim that Scripture and tradition are potentially infinite. It is even difficult to understand the claim that Scripture and tradition "belong to the semantic field in which images of the divine are embedded." A given image may fall within a larger semantic field, but I cannot think how Scripture and tradition can be said to "belong to" a semantic field.

11. There is some ambiguity here, since on p. 87 she suggests that both the ontological and confessional components of her definition of God are given in Scripture and tradition, the only confessional sources we have. That would seem to undermine a distinction between ontological and confessional. Is she distinguishing between God's being in se and deus pro nobis? Is the immanent Trinity ontological and the economic Trinity confessional? If presence (to extra-trinitarian subjects) is part of God's being the answer to both questions would be no.

12. Schertz also offers as a reason for appealing to Scripture that "logic indicates" that it is in Scripture and tradition that "images of the divine are embedded" (p. 86). Why does logic indicate this? Are not images of the divine also embedded in Native American and Goddess religions?

13.  Schertz is right to say that models of God
need not be restricted to those explicitly contained within Scripture.  The Reformed theologians,
for example, talked of the gubernatio dei, and
Lutherans of the deus absconditus.  Both are
appropriate, within limits, though neither is mentioned in Scripture.  On the other hand, God as
causa prima is probably inappropriate. We need
criteria of appropriateness--authorizing criteria--
and not just criteria of possibility. While I am
critical of Schertz's argument, I am not opposed to
thinking or speaking of God as friend; such speech
has a long tradition in evangelical circles in an
effort to personalize relationship with God.

14.  It is tempting to think of Jephthah's
daughter in christological terms.  However, the
pact that led to her sacrifice only perpetuated the
cycle of violence of which it was a part.  Following the Ammonite slaughter (Judges 11:33), forty-
two thousand Ephraimites fell to Jephthah's Gilea-
dites (12:6).  Her story does not change the course
of the narrative; it is a telling parenthesis within it.

# METHOD AND UNDERSTANDING FOR TEXTS AND DISCIPLES

## Willard M. Swartley

Since one respondent to the above section
declined her assignment at a late date, I have felt
it appropriate to write a response as one of the
editors of the volume. Writing at this time, I
also have had the opportunity to reflect upon Ben
Ollenburger's response. This has also influenced
my thought in the conversational quest to understand the texts which Mary Schertz has chosen for
the three Bible studies and the complementary essay
by David Schroeder. I am also aware that both
Schertz and Schroeder have continued to work on
these specific papers, expanding and refining them
significantly.

The focus I propose, as my title indicates, is
the relation between method and understanding. Do
the methods which Schroeder and Schertz employ contribute to a genuine understanding of the text (and
here I assume that ascertaining authorial intention
is the primary task of exegesis which in turn leads
to understanding)? Or does the Schroeder/Schertz
exegesis and its results produce a certain tension
between their proposed understandings of the text
and the text itself? This question applies to all
three levels of the exegetical and hermeneutical
process: says, means, and significance.[1]

Regarding method generally, it is correct in my
judgment to begin with the literary analysis and
then utilize the findings that arise from an investigation into the historical background, as a
secondary and contributing source of clarification.
Hence, I will focus first on Schertz's analysis of
1 Peter 2 and 3. Schertz has demonstrated well how
the analysis of structure can help us understand
what lies at the heart of given pericope (esp.
2:21-24). By pointing out that Jesus' non-
retaliatory model in 2:23—and specifically 23b,
"when he suffered he did not threaten," is the center of the chiastic ring composition of that crucial "paradigm" paragraph, Schertz proposes that
this provides the clue for understanding the
parallel units:

Community's Relation to Human (Political)
Institutions (2:13-17)
Slaves' Relation to (Overbearing) Masters
(2:18-20)
            The CHRIST MODEL (2:21-24)
Wives   Relation   to   (Unbelieving)   Husbands
(3:1-6)
General for Believers, Good-doing in Relation
to Evil-doing (3:8-17)

This   analysis   is   impressive   and   raises one
point   of   observation   and one of   inquiry.   First,
3:7 in addressing husbands does not neatly fit into
the   analysis;   it   stands somewhat in tension with
the   social   structural pattern evident in the other
pericopae.   Second, in what way does the structural
analysis   disclose   or   illumine   the text, and thus
enable   our   understanding?   Schertz's   proposed
understanding   of   the   text   posits parallelism of
thought   in   each   of   these   five   units, with the
Christ-model   hymn,   and   its   strategic   center in
verse   23b,   providing   the   clue   to the essential
theological and moral directive that determines the
shape   of   the   response   in   all   cases.   It   is
theological   in   that   Christ's   behavior shows the
divine   will and way; it is moral directive in that
in   every   pericope   the   author   gives   behavioral
exhortation.
Ollenburger's critique, however, indicates that
Schertz's   analysis   does   not   convince   the reader
that   the   first   and   fourth units are of the same
essential   character   as   the   other   three.   The
believers'   subjection   to political human institutions   and   the   subjection of wives to unbelieving
husbands   are   not   shown   to be responses to evil.
Further,   Ollenburger   does   not   see   in Schertz's
analysis   nor   in   the biblical text any indication
that   these   institutions   are   evil;   only the abuse
of   relationships   within   the structures are evil--
but even that must be inferred in these texts.
Behind   Schertz's work and Ollenburger's critique   may   lie also, I propose, differing understandings   of   the   rhetorical   method   and   what may be
validly deduced from its findings.   For Schertz the
evidence that may be deduced from ring   composition
appears   to be greater and more decisive than Ollenburger   allows.   Thus   Schertz, in following a basic

axiom of this method, assumes that what is evident
in the decisive central unit of a ring composition,
is true also of the other enclosing units, i.e.,
once parallelism of thought is the formative factor
in the structural composition. Hence, Schertz's
analysis assumes that response to evil is the
prevailing issue throughout all five units. Ollenburger is not persuaded of this point, and queries
whether this point doesn't efface what the text
actually says. To resolve such differing judgment
about what a text says and means, I suggest further
textual study.

An additional aspect of literary analysis may
help to clarify and, in my judgment, strengthen
Schertz's contribution. Belonging to any model of
literary, structural or rhetorical analysis, is the
factor of repetition and use of key terms. Significantly, the terms "evil and good" (with
variants of evil- or good-doing) occur in partial
or complete parallelism a dozen times within the
segment under study (and some of these Schertz has
noted in her later fuller version). The list is as
follows:

-Maintain good conduct... so that when accused
of evil-doing they will see your good works (2:12)

-Governors are to punish evil-doers and praise
good-doers; by being subject and doing good you put
to shame the ignorance of foolish humans (same word
as in v.13 to desribe the human institution) (2:14-
15)

-God approves enduring suffering for good doing
but not for sinning (2:20)

-(note verse 23 as parallel thought, but with
the terms not reviling when reviled and not
threatening when suffering)

-Wives are to be good doers and not be ter-
rified, presumably by evil treatment (3:6)

-Do not return evil for evil...but rather bless
(3:9)

-He who sees good days keeps his lips from
speaking evil (3:10)

-Turn away from evil and do good (3:11)

-The Lord regards the righteous..but is against
those doing evil (3:12)

-Who is there to do evil against you if you are
zealous for the good (3:13)

-By keeping a clear conscience when abused

those who <u>revile</u> you for <u>good</u> in Christ are shamed
(3:16)

-It is better to suffer for doing <u>good</u> than for
doing <u>evil</u> (3:17)

The permeation of this <u>good</u> (<u>agathos</u>) and <u>evil</u>
(<u>kakos</u>) vocabulary throughout the segment quite
clearly indicates that this is the dominant theme
of this particular text. The fact that the
terminology occurs in each of the five sub-units
indicates also the author's intention, namely, that
a particular kind of conduct, i.e., <u>doing good</u>, is
called for in the context of others doing <u>evil</u> to
us. The text focuses, however, not on any of the
institutions <u>per se</u>, but in the way in which the
institutions and relationships express themselves.
The situation envisioned by the epistle is that of
believers experiencing evil in each of the circumstances: believers from authorities, slaves from
masters and wives from husbands. The central unit
provides the model for Christian response and the
last a general warranting summary.

Granted, the text does not explicitly say that
authorities do evil; they are rather to punish the
evil-doers. But the following verse (15) infers as
much in its call for doing good to silence ignorant
foolish humans, especially since the word <u>human</u>
(<u>anthropon</u>) echoes <u>human</u> (<u>anthropine</u>) institution
of verse 13. Similarly, in the fourth unit, the
juxtaposition of <u>doing good</u> and the command not to
fear any <u>terrifying</u> act or intimidation (3:6)
strongly infers <u>evil-doing</u> on the part of those
husbands who do "not obey the word" (v. 1).

The significance of this investigation is thus
two-fold: on the one hand, a direct correlation
between the findings of this literary method of
study and the nature of the moral mandate for
believers to do good in return for evil can be
maintained. Second, the text itself gives no warrant for extrapolating from this particular situation in order to define the moral nature of any of
the institutions under discussion. However, the
recurrence of the <u>good for evil</u> motif throughout
this section <u>and</u> the careful structural arrangement
when taken together leads to an understanding of
this text that holds, on the one hand, that evil is
experienced by believers within the relational
structures of these institutions and, on the other,

that a specific Christian pattern of response is
prescribed. It is also clear that the institutions
as such are not given moral mandate but by
inference are held accountable to moral criteria of
good and evil. In my judgment, this theological
perspective enables the "oppressed" one not to be
victim but to be the willing bearer of moral power
that has as its aim "overcoming evil with good."
This then is the Christian moral strategy by which
to change structures that oppress humans.

Within the context of this analysis, Schroeder's historical reconstruction provides verifica-
tion for the findings of the literary investigation. However, his judgment--based upon his analysis of the household--that women choosing Christianity was a subversive act in relation to the
patriarchal structure of the household is the type
of judgment that falls somewhere between the
explicit warrants of the historical reconstruction
and the information of the biblical text. In my
own estimation, it is a correct inference and
stands scores high on the probability graph. That
judgment can either be verified or proven false by
additional extra-biblical data or further clearer
understandings from ongoing literary study of the
biblical texts.

Finally, let us note that Schertz' selection of
this text and study of it was to illustrate one of
three ways feminist biblical scholars are doing
biblical study in order to enable the biblical
tradition to empower feminist concerns. This study
aimed to show how study of texts about women can
function to counteract the use of famous texts
"against" women. Indeed, 1 Peter 3:1-6 has often
been used, even by Christian men and women, to
remind wives of their subordinate status and function to husbands. Further, the point has often
been extended to include all women in relation to
men. Similarly, 2:13-17 has sometimes been used to
argue for an indiscriminate obedience to government
authority. These studies and comments above show
that this is not the best use of the text in fidel-
ity to the intentions of the text-message in its
historical setting? The main point of this segment
of Scripture is to call men and women to follow the
Christ-model in oppressive situations.

## II. The Lukan Study on Authority

Schertz undertook the Lukan study to illustrate a second method by which feminist biblical scholars find the biblical text to empower feminist concerns, namely to show how looking to the biblical text generally can offer a theological perspective that critiques patriarchy. Indeed, a cursory reading of Luke 19:28-21:38 would hardly strike anyone as a text in which one might find a critique of patriarchy, especially since all the human characters of the plot are male. When, however, one focuses on the respective roles of authority that the different characters in the plot carry, the potential for critique of structural power emerges. Schertz's stated rationale for pursuing this study is that the issues of power and authority are central both to this text and to feminist concerns. Hence, by analogy the findings will be applied to the power issue inherent in patriarchal structures.

As I observed in my comments on 1 Peter, other levels of literary analysis might further enrich and broaden the answers to the understandings which Schertz gains from this particular text.

Here I make two literary observations: first, the response of the disciples (those who carry third order of authority according to Schertz) stands in antiphonal relationship to the heavenly angelic song at the beginning of Luke's main narrative: The angels' praise, "peace on earth" in 2:14, receives here its antiphonal response from the disciples' outcry, "peace in heaven." The text stresses the necessity for someone to speak this response; if not, the very stones will cry it out. This emphasizes the urgency and overwhelming significance of the kingdom's manifestation in this stage of Jesus' ministry. The second observation is that Jesus' statement about "the things that make for peace" consummates another important redactional Lukan theme, namely the use of the word peace which, occurring 14 times in Luke, stands in stark$_3$ contrast to its rare use in both Matthew and Mark.

When the roles of the different categories of authority are thus noted, a further observation emerges as well. The latter three categories of authority function in opposition to the first category, that of the religious leaders: first, the multitude of people, including disciples generally, thwart what the officers are seeking to do; second the disciples, including here the appointed followers of Jesus specifically, participate in the divine human drama of the Gospel's plot and purpose in crying out this word of praise; and third, Jesus himself has ultimate authority and carries forward this plot and purpose to its end, even at the cost of rejection and death at the hands of the rulers, desertion by those who followed generally and denial by those closest to him.

What can we learn then by the use of this particular method of literary analysis? It is important, in my judgment, to put each given text into dialogue with the larger purposes of a given book as disclosed by analysis of its literary structure, overall plot, and dominant themes. To illustrate further: when Schertz raises the question at the end about how this text relates to women, she moves from the text to this gathering of women convened to study the Bible and feminist issues in light of Scripture. This, she sees, as indeed a sign of hope that women figure into the story even though women are not present in the text of study. However, an intermediate and more closely linked textual point could have been made. One of Luke's overall literary emphases accents the significant role of women in the narrative, so much so that it would be appropriate to suggest at least that in this very text women were among the disciples who echoed the antiphonal response, "peace in heaven." This point embraces also then the Luke 2 drama and thus includes the significant role of Mary as the larger context for the Luke 19 narrative. By taking into account this larger structural dimension to themes consummated in Luke 19, women are not only an inferred part of Luke's strategic antiphonal praise, "Peace in heaven," but they are in their identification with Mary and her role in the salvation drama a very substantial part of doing those "things that make for peace." For clearly, Mary's child and God's child emerges in this narrative as the voice and person who understands and represents the peace of God, even when in collision with people in the structures of power who by their power have become blinded to God's ways.

Reflecting upon these two essays together, women emerge in exemplary roles in the Christian story: substantial participation in God's salvation drama and modeling the Christ-type, <u>doing good</u> in response to evil. If we were to include the Jephthah story also, we could add: grieving over moral atrocities that arise from human religious zeal even with God-incurred sanction.[4]

## Notes

1.  These are the three stages of hermeneutical analysis outlined by Perry Yoder in his study, From Word to Life: A Guide to the Art of Bible Study (Scottdale, Pa.: Herald Press, 1982), 31-51.

2.  From Katherine Doob Sakenfeld, "Feminist Uses of Biblical Material," in Feminist Interpretation of the Bible, ed. Letty M. Russell (Philadelphia: Westminster, 1985), 55-64.

3.  See my essay, "Politics and Peace (Eirene) in Luke's Gospel," in Political Issues in Luke-Acts, ed. Richard J.. Cassidy and Philip J. Scharper (Maryknoll, NY: Orbis Books, 1983), 18-37.

4.  For this last study, on which I will forego comment since I have little to add to Ollenburger's response, Schertz seeks to illustrate the third type of feminist study of Scripture noted by Sakenfeld, i.e., "looking to texts about women to learn from the history and stories of ancient and modern women who live in patriarchal cultures" (ibid., 62-63). The primary purpose of this type of study is not to forget them/us--to remember both their anguish and their triumphs. Inspired by Phyllis Trible's work in Texts of Terror, Schertz uses the Jephthah story to illustrate this method of feminist hermeneutic. With Ollenburger, I find it difficult to understand why this text was chosen to develop the metaphor of God as Friend. Is it a call to feel God's pathos amid such human tragedy and experience divine friendship in the face of excruciating grief and foolish male military heroism in which the loveliest and dearest are sacrificed for "righteous" causes?

# RESPONSE TO THE RESPONDERS

## Mary Schertz

I am grateful for the dialogue that has been a consequence of the three studies I presented at the consultation on feminist hermeneutics. Both the assent and the dissent as well as the expansion and qualification of my ideas have been extremely helpful in my own process of clarifying these issues. I am happy to have an opportunity to respond to a part of that dialogue.

## I. Response to Swartley

Swartley does a fine job of raising the significant discussion issues. With respect to his comments on the 1 Peter material, I will respond briefly to his point of observation and then a bit more fully to his point of inquiry.

Swartley's observation that the address to husbands in 3:7 "does not neatly fit into the analysis" is a correct observation. That is a problem. It is, however, a problem for most analyses of this text, the more traditional ones as well as the more methodologically innovative. To Swartley's comment that this address stands in social tension with the other pericopae, one could add that it also stands in some rhetorical tension with its surrounding material. Is it an aside? A parenthesis? An afterthought? A corrective to an anticipated misunderstanding of 3:1-6? The question of how 3:7 fits with its context is an important one, one not adequately addressed in either my study or most others, whether rhetorical, sociological or historical. Perhaps future scholarship on 1 Peter will resolve this issue.

Swartley's inquiry into the relationship between method and the illumination of the issue of evildoing and good-doing central to this section of the text is very helpful. I think it might be worthwhile to point out here that the observations of the relationships of parallelism evident in this text are hardly original. Many scholars have noticed the pattern of the _general_ injunction about government, the _specific_ injunction to slaves, the _specific_ injunction to wives and the _general_ injunction to return good for evil. My contribution to the discussion is a perception that the

Christ-model hymn in 2:21-24 centers and organizes
this pattern. Swartley's further work with the
repetitive use of such terms as evildoing and good-
doing is particularly constructive and, as he says,
strengthens the point I am making about the text.
His work with these terms is especially useful at a
point of caution I raised in the original study. I
noted there that the relationship between human
institution - "masters" - tormentors - "husbands" -
evil on the one hand and community - slave- Christ
- wives - good on the other hand should not be
"oversimplified." While the symmetry and care with
which the units are related would indicate that the
author sees analogies between these concepts, these
analogies are certainly not simple equations.
Swartley's emphasis that the author is advocating a
particular response to be assumed by the readers
when they encounter evil in these institutions
rather than defining the moral nature of the
institutions themselves is, I think, a very important point. The question about what sort of critique is offered these institutions by the author's
development and advocacy of a not-returning-in-kind
response to the evil within them should begin with
Swartley's emphasis that they "are not given moral
mandate but by inference are held accountable to
moral criteria of good and evil."

With respect to Swartley's comments on the
study of the Lucan material, I am in wholehearted
agreement that the issues of power and authority in
the passage with which I was working need to be
studied in conjunction with the passage's larger
literary setting in Luke-Acts. I appreciate the
suggestions Swartley makes about how this larger
task might be initiated and would want to take his
suggestions seriously in any further work.

One cautionary note that I would raise in relation to this issue has to do with the literary role
of women in Luke-Acts. While I would like very
much to agree with Swartley that this role is positive, Elisabeth Schüssler Fiorenza's comments to
the contrary are weighty enough in my opinion to
put the burden of proof on those who would argue
for a positive view. This issue is, of course, a
vital one for studies of this gospel and part of
the reason Lucan studies are attracting such lively
interest from New Testament scholars at present. I

look forward to significant development in these
issues in the near future.

## II. Response to Ollenburger

This response to Ollenburger's paper will
involve addressing first a point of misperception,
secondly two points of clarification and, finally,
a point of appreciation and discussion.

The point of misperception is that the goal of
the study on 1 Peter is "to disarm the text of its
offensive possibilities by proposing interpretations in which the text supports, rather than
opposes, those positions we have come to hold."
This goal describes neither the intent nor the
result of the study.

The stated goal of the paper is instead "to
look to texts about women to counteract famous
texts used 'against' women." While one strand of
feminist hermeneutics assumes this task as a
mandate to prove that the NT documents are essentially feminist documents which have been patriar-
chally misinterpreted, it is not a dominant position and it is not one to which I ascribe. A better description of the mandate of this particular
task of feminist hermeneutics would be the use of a
suspicion of historically patriarchal interpretation as an heuristic tool in order to better understand what the text says. In other words, the goal
of feminist interpretation shares the larger goal
of all biblical scholarship using, as does all biblical scholarship, a certain set of understandings
as a tool to meet that goal.

Thus the hermeneutical intent of my work on 1
Peter is much more modest than Ollenburger sup-
poses. The injunction to the wives in 1 Peter has
been used to justify women's subordination in the
church as well as more generally. My counteraction
of that usage is limited to my observation that a
close rhetorical analysis of the text does not, in
my opinion, support the subordination of either
slaves or wives within the communities of Christians to which it is addressed. The subordination
instruction to slaves and wives assumes these
slaves and wives to be members of non-Christian
households as well as belonging to the new
"household" of the Christian community. The
rhetorical arrangement of the material clarifies

that these injunctions are to be obeyed in the context of the members' relations with their non-
Christian households. The rhetorical arrangement
would, by contrast, indicate that the subordination
of the "younger" to the "elder" does apply to the
internal structure of the Christian "households."
Therefore, the result of the study is also quite
modest: It would seem inappropriate to use this
text to justify continuing class or gender domination among the people of God. It would not be
inappropriate to use this text to justify the
establishment or maintenance of a hierarchical
arrangement based upon maturity or religious experience in the Christian community.

A point of clarification has to do with Ollenburger's comment (p. 99) that my 1 Peter research
"makes no mention of the historical and social context." Literary critics of the NT are commonly
accused of being ahistorical when, in fact, this is
not the case. The literature studied by NT
literary critics is ancient literature which functioned in specific social contexts. Of course historical and social concerns are of great interest.
The omission in this case is not methodological but
pragmatic, since Schroeder's paper was also on the
program.

A second point of clarification has to do with
Ollenburger's question of whether Christian theology can be "satisfied" with rhetorical strategy as
a reason to take Scripture and tradition into
account in "constructive theology." Since a major
task of Christian theology is to make the connections between the scriptural tradition and theology, I would certainly hope that Christian theology
would not be "satisfied" with this reason or any
other. This reason is a reason consonant with the
task at hand, however, which is why it is cited.
Other, and presumably better reasons are not pre-
cluded.

While there are some other points which could
be raised in a corrective mode and while there are
a number of items which could be discussed quite
profitably and enjoyably, I will limit the discussion here to that item for which I have the
greatest appreciation. Ollenburger's questions
about the daughter of Jephthah story are important
ones and ones which need to be held in tension with

Trible's interpretation. To read this story as a
stark account of victimization in which God, the
victimizer, and the victim all conspire by various
actions and inactions to accomplish the destruction
is a valid reading of the text, a point which
serves to illustrate the principle that all interpretation is a work of interaction between the text
and the interpreter. Interpreters with different
perceptions, different experiences and different
social situations can and will interpret texts differently. Obviously, Trible is approaching this
text with a notion that oppressed people sometimes
make moral distinctions, choices and statements
that are not always apparent to their oppressors or
even to the transmitters of their traditions, often
perhaps for reasons of survival. Trible then uses
this principle of oppression theory heuristically
as she studies the text and tries to understand it
better. While approaching texts from the stand-
point of oppression theory does not guarantee
accuracy, such an approach should, it seems to me,
be granted a serious hearing among a people who
take the ideal of servanthood to heart.

III.    The Daughter of Jepthah as a Narrative Component of God as Friend
        Both the written responses and the responses of
the persons attending the consultation have
prompted me to reflect further upon the question of
why I have chosen the somewhat unlikely story of
Jephthah's daughter to complement the model of God
as Friend. In that process, I have concluded that
what Trible's exegesis of the story and my use of
it in the construction of God as Friend both point
toward is a level of experience which presumes
activism and asks what lies beyond it. In other
words, we might conceptualize the struggle for justice in at least three stages. There is the pre-
critical stage:   one does not see the injustice
whether perpetrated against oneself or others.
Because no problem is perceived, no action is
taken.    There is the critical stage:  one's consciousness is raised, one is angry and active.
This stage is described quite eloquently by Ollenburger as a time of unfurled wrath and lifted
voices. Then there is the post-critical stage.
One is at this point not uncritical. One is, in

fact, fully committed to protest. Every day that
one lives is an action of protest, every word one
speaks a word of protest. The unfurled wrath or
the lifted voice is at this point not a decision;
it is a life.

The problem, it seems to me, is that if one
lives one's life in the context of this commitment,
one comes in time to understand that despite
protest, despite activism of the most profound
sort, one will nevertheless continue to live one's
life and die one's death in the context of that
which one is protesting and against which one is
acting. Not only do we live within the context of
patriarchalism, racism, militarism, and economic
exploitation, but we live diminished lives within
these contexts. These structures waste us--sapping
our energy, resources and creativity as well as our
capacity for love. Perceiving these realities is
not a passive response because one arrives at this
level of despair only through commitment to and
practice of activism. The question presented
starkly by the nuclear threat, but just as real in
other structures of oppression, is how to go on
living after we acknowledge that the forces
diminishing us will continue to diminish us and our
children and our children's children. For example,
when we, as feminists committed to protest and
action, know that we have no choice but to live our
lives within a patriarchal society which diminishes
us, then the question becomes how do we wrest meaning from this absurdity? What is responsibility
and what is hope in the face of the persistence of
these evils despite our continued best efforts?

It is precisely at this point that the daughter
of Jephthah constructed as a model of God as Friend
speaks to me, and we could do far worse than to be
guided by her. First, we can determine with her
not to be morally controlled by the forces against
us. We can decide not to return the evil; we can
decide to remain "present" with our oppressors, and
refuse to objectify them. We do not need to act
like them. In other words, we can decide to offer
and to keep on offering the bases of friendship,
knowing that the growth and development of those
friendships depend on the responses of the "other."
That "minimal" action at least leaves open the possibility of friendship--reconciliation, reform,

etc. In the words of Romans, we have at least done what we can "in so far as it depends on us" to live at peace.

Second, and beyond that, we can and must find others; we must end our isolation and get together on the mountain to befriend one another. We must be God as Friend to one another--for thus we survive, thus we create meaning in the midst of meaninglessness, thus we strengthen ourselves that we might continue to protest and to act against the structures of destruction. This befriending develops the bases of friendship, presence and subject-regard, into bonds that transcend the limitations and dichotomies imposed upon us by the structures of dominance.

In this sense, the daughter's consent to her father is not a lack of protest but a profound refusal to see him as less than a moral subject like herself. In this sense, the daughter's gathering on the mountain is not withdrawal, but ekklesia.

As for constructing God in her image, again we could do far worse. It seems to me that it might be helpful to think about God thus: Her very Body, our earth, jeopardized by our unholy alliances with "foolish male military heroism," God nevertheless refuses to retreat from Her regard of us as subjects. At the same time, this God calls those of us who dare to be Her friends into ekklesia on the mountain. There on the mountain the anger burns bright--and so does the love. There we are renewed and nurtured and from there we return--to fight once more the fight whose victory we will not live to see but which we must wage anyway in order to befriend ourselves, our friends and our Friend.

BS680.W7 P47x                    c.1
                                  100105  000
Perspectives on feminist herme

3 9310 00084564 2
GOSHEN COLLEGE-GOOD LIBRARY